ALONE IN COLIN'S COTTAGE

BY JUNE SUTTON

June Sutton's published work includes serials, novels and short stories. Amateur groups have publicly performed her one-act plays whilst her stories have been broadcast on BBC radio. She is a member of The Society of Authors, Romantic Novelists' Association and The Society of Women Writers and Journalists. She is also President and Founder of Facing It Together groups for the widowed in Norfolk. Alone in Colin's Cottage is the book she wrote whilst living alone in her isolated home for six years, coming to terms with the death of her husband.

Published by Boldface Press,
www.linguasy.com/boldface
boldface@linguasy.com

First published, 2000.

Alone in Colin's Cottage by June Sutton
ISBN 0-646-39204-2
Autobiography; Bereavement

Cover illustration by Colin Sutton; design by Paul Sutton

Dedication: For Paul, Seán and Martin.

ACKNOWLEDGEMENTS

Colin Murray Parkes OBE MD DPM FRCPsych, Founder and President of Cruse Bereavement Care, for his invaluable help and advice after reading a draft of the book.

Cruse Bereavement Care for their article, "Sexual Feelings After The Death Of A Partner" from the Chronicle. Cruse address: 126 Sheen Road, Richmond, Surrey TW9 1UR.

Leo Marks for his beautiful poem, "The Life That I Have", used in the film, "Carve Her Name With Pride".

The late Michael Bentine C.B.E. for his lively and uplifting phone calls and permission to quote, "Anything of mine".

New English Bible © Oxford University Press and Cambridge University Press 1961, 1970.

The Samaritans who provide confidential, emotional support for anyone in crisis, twenty-four hours a day, every day of the year. Wherever you are in the UK you can call 08457 90 90 90 for the cost of a local call. (1850 60 90 90 in the Republic of Ireland).

Members of the Aylsham Facing It Together group, Norfolk for allowing me to use their experiences to help others.

Journalist, Jack Barfoot, Chairman '97 - '99 Sutton Writers' Circle, Surrey, for his patient copy reading and unstinting encouragement.

My beloved family without whom there would be no book.

ALONE IN COLIN'S COTTAGE

BY

JUNE SUTTON

PREFACE

There is no right time to die. No right way. Death is not the adventure. Life is the adventure.

I didn't want the adventure of living in an isolated cottage. Not along a mile of muddy track. But I did live there. I certainly didn't want to be left alone there for six years. But I was.

We did all sorts with that cottage: renovated, reared livestock, built a nuclear bunker and... it turned out to be fun. But when we first exchanged suburbia for The Good Life, my stress ratings went soaring into sensational sunsets. Then, slowly, I became seduced by gold and silver seasons - until five minutes of hell turned Paradise into Purgatory.

When I was bereaved, I thought no one could have ever felt like I did. In a way that's right because we all grieve differently. And until it happens to us we cannot imagine the devastation. I had never wept so much or felt such raw despair.

Apart from exhaustion and apathy there can be proper aches and pains. Perhaps we are left sexually adrift. We may feel angry, frightened or guilty or experience loss of control. I simply found the sheer effort of living a tremendous ordeal for a long time.

There are wonderful stories of people battling their way through shadows with great courage and stiff upper lip. But for every step forward I seemed to topple two back. Sobbing into streams. And clinging to trees.

Until, with much help, I found my way of coping.

Alone in Colin's Cottage is in memory of my gifted husband who I will love always. It is for our sons, Paul, Seán and Martin. And for the children who will never know him.

And it is especially for anyone mourning the loss of a loved one. You are not alone.

PART ONE

ONE

The derelict cottage crouched in the crutch of green-stained undergrowth. Surrounding it, wide wet fields stretched to a bleak flat nowhere.

He had to be kidding...

Wasn't he?

I must take some of the blame. The year before we'd holidayed in Yorkshire. I was awe-struck by craggy splendour. Streams glugged, sheep grazed by the front door and trout darted deliciously in unpolluted waters.

'Wouldn't it be marvellous to live in the country?' I sighed. I said it to the wrong guy.

'Then let's go for it... we only live once!' he said. Much too immediately.

I was obviously drunk with sunshine and scenery. After all, I liked high heels, well-lit tarmac pavements, people and shopping. I had grown up on an estate in Derby where communing with nature consisted of trampling down nearby allotments or day-trips to Dovedale.

Colin's childhood was spent at Freshwater on the Isle of Wight. He was always going on about his granny's farmhouse where walls were hung with salty sides of bacon and drooling strings of fat brown onions.

I knew married life with him would not be conventional but I was soppy about him and didn't care. Our homes ranged from living on an island in the Thames to a solitary shack in a wood, to a cottage in Cornwall built on to the rock-face. When we finally settled in a semi-detached near Norwich his alliance with suburbia was not as easy as mine.

Colin continued to chew on the remark I'd made and we were soon scouring Norfolk for Utopia. So was everyone else.

Mention of mortgages was the kiss of death. Cottages ripe for conversion were snapped up by those with ready cash to slap down. And there was always someone with inside information who reached a property before we did. But it livened up weekends and we got to see all the pretty villages squatting between the Broads.

Winter tightened and I went right off the whole idea. Holidays were a long time ago.

Weeks before I'd had an article published about being gazumped. Now I received a letter from a reader to say she had a cottage she'd sell but doubted we'd be interested because of its position. Too true, I thought, after reading her description and filed away the memory. Colin didn't. He was addicted. He'd look at anything. He went to see it one day when I was in bed with flu.

'It's marvellous,' he enthused. 'You'd love it. I could do wonders if I could only get my hands on it.'

'You didn't tell me you were going to see it,' I croaked. I'm irritable when I'm not very well. Like my father, Colin used to say.

'You know you have to be quick off the mark.'

'It's probably sold already,' I said hopefully.

'It's not. I spoke to the owner. We're the first to know about it!'

It was April Fools' Day, 1977, when we drove along the Cromer road in blinding rain. Soon we were bumping for three-quarters of a mile along a narrow unmade track called a "loke". We continued to lurch and splash through puddles and potholes, the grey Norfolk landscape trailing each side of us.

'You wait,' Colin said. As if there was a big box of chocolates coming my way.

We turned sharply. The loke became even narrower and more over-grown. Blackthorn hedges scraped spiteful nails across our windows. When the way ahead was totally choked we clambered from the car.

And that's when I saw it. The cottage. I'm not sure what I expected. Compensation for that loke maybe. Roses round the door or a thatched roof. Even a bird tweeting.

It looked like a broken box. Rotting window frames decorated with shards of glass hung from gaps in the brickwork. Ivy crept across cracks, crevices and loose roof tiles that begged in the biting wind. One chimney had a great gaping gash and the other leaned sympathetically towards it. Only an ugly disused power pole a few feet from the cottage reminded us there had once been life in that dismal spot.

It was a truly desolate sight.

I turned to stare at Colin. He was smiling. He wasn't seeing what I was seeing. But then he was a visionary. An artist.

We struggled with a heap of firewood that had once been a gate. The front door hanging from broken hinges refused to admit us so we squeezed through the kitchen window into the cottage, sliding over skeletal remains left by foxes.

Colin dug a penknife into woodwork in the two-up-two-down rooms, murmuring, 'Look at that… dry as a bone.' I didn't take any notice. I wasn't going to live in the God-forsaken place.

Seán and Martin, our two younger sons, sixteen and twelve, visited the cottage that evening and decided it was 'Great.' You could shoot rabbits from bedroom windows.

Great.

Colin had dark brown eyes that could eat you and a soft seductive voice. He looked at me earnestly, 'If you want to give it a try, I'll build you a place you'll love - and if you don't like it in a couple of years we'll sell up and move. Or just say the word and we'll forget the whole idea.'

Forget it! screamed my subconscious. Why couldn't I say it?

'Think about it,' he said quietly.

Paul, our eldest son had not seen the place. At nineteen there were far more delightful things to do than delving into deserted properties every weekend. But the others told him all about it.

'Sounds great,' he said.

There are times when a woman needs a daughter.

Colin's job was designing and supervising the building of other people's dream homes and he was obviously excited at the thought of designing his own. He wooed me with superb dream-cottage plans, but whenever I thought about it, the loke grew longer. A mile of potholes was not conducive to casual callers. I could become a social leper. I dreamed of the isolated cottage shrouded in mists and before you could say, 'Wuthering Heights', I started sleepwalking. Sleep-running would be more exact. But when morning came, shadows vanished and reason took over. Colin was right, this was a once-in-a-lifetime opportunity. Cottages for renovation were certainly very scarce. And how could I possibly know if I wouldn't like living there if I didn't try it?

'OK, I'll give it a couple of years,' I finally said. He kept asking me if I was sure I didn't want to change my mind and if he'd asked just once more I would've done.

When we visited the cottage again, sunshine bathed its mellow red brick walls and hedges around were juicily green. Spring is the best estate agent of them all.

That evening I read an article in the Eastern Daily Press about a woman whose family persuaded her to move into the country where she found it unbearably lonely and became an alcoholic.

TWO

Everyone was an expert:

'The best way of taking water to that cottage, mate, is to tap from the mains.'

'No, Colin, you want a bore-hole, it's cheaper and you'll be laughing in a drought.'

'You should subcontract out all the work at the cottage.'

'You get an estimate from one firm to do the lot, Colin.'

A property without water, power or drains proved a great challenge to Colin's colleagues in the building industry. They shovelled out advice.

As with most things he looked into all aspects calmly and logically.

My friends teased me about becoming a hermit. I laughed it off and then bit my fingernails ragged. Blow all that stuff about logic. But later I reasoned you can be lonely wherever you live. People cocoon themselves. I once had a miscarriage whilst I was alone in a house in a built-up area. Most neighbours were out working and I stupidly felt I did not know others well enough to ask for help. Only the arrival of an ambulance alerted them.

Sometimes we make our own loneliness.

On the surface Colin appeared to be mild mannered. However, he was strongly stirred by such topics as planet pollution, could be derisive of banal television - and was not happy with the pious. But he was generally enormously patient, especially in his job, which wasn't always easy, as in the case of one client who insisted he designed her bathroom with a bidet three long strides from the lavatory because it looked nicer.

He was just as unruffled with me when I wanted rooms switched around on the final cottage layout. He'd drawn lots of designs, each more tempting than its predecessor... 'Just to give you an idea of what the place could look like.' And then came the layout no one in her right mind would turn down.

'Is it too late now for changes?' I said, knowing it was time to put in for planning.

'Don't worry, most women change their minds up to the very last minute, but you can't have every room facing south,' he said evenly, pencil poised.

The application went in. Suddenly daydreams were sneaking towards reality.

Twelve cats living next door to our semi-detached began ravaging the garden, tipping over dustbins, scratching up vegetables and salivating over the outside aviary, killing several birds.

'Cats are classed as vermin,' the Health Inspector said. 'Can't do anything about cats.'

After more murders, Colin began creeping around with a catapult. For the first time, I felt the pull of an isolated cottage.

When we put our home up for sale, the first viewer said, 'I live in the country, dear. My God. The silence out there! I can't wait to get back to civilisation.'

Anticipating a sale we searched for a property to rent while the cottage was to be renovated. We found nothing. We weren't going to appease wary landlords by getting rid of our small mongrel dog, Jess or any of our sons.

'What about a caravan on site?' I suggested.

'Not in the winter. You wouldn't like that.' Colin looked at me dubiously… 'But there is somewhere…' He'd been offered temporary use of Homestead, an old house due for demolition. A small estate was to be built in its grounds.

'Been empty for ages… in a bit of a state.'

I didn't care. It was somewhere to live. Colin took me to see it.

Wallpaper hung in long wet strips like last year's bunting. There were no power points upstairs so we'd concentrate on making downstairs habitable. Apart from two small living rooms, downstairs had an interesting extension with a drain, a tap hanging drunkenly in the middle of one wall and a sloping concrete floor where anaemic stinging nettles had taken root. Adjoining was a dark little scullery containing a cupboard full of rat droppings. A cracked white sink faced a graffiti-daubed wall. Other walls and doors were coated with thick lumps of rancid lard.

'Won't take long if we get cracking.'

We scrubbed, wallpapered, made bonfires, disinfected and attacked the lavatory with a penknife.

By now permission had been given for repairs to begin on the cottage-roof before bad weather could cause further deterioration. If we tapped from the mains water supply at the end of the loke it would be our responsibility to take water as far as the cottage.

We enquired about the upkeep of the loke and were told a farmer might throw a few stones down from time to time. This was partly true - I did once see a cartload of stones and rotten carrots tipped on it.

Colin was really eager to get cracking on the cottage at last and proud to own a property of character with a sizeable chunk of land; more than we'd ever had. One day he was talking to a couple who were having a large country house built. The wife argued with her husband.

'But we don't want a big garden. No one has big gardens these days.' She turned to Colin, 'How big is your garden?'

He tried to sound nonchalant, 'An acre.'

'There you are,' cried the wife triumphantly, 'no one has big gardens any more.'

We exchanged contracts in September. I must have hesitated because the solicitor whispered to me, 'do I detect a certain reluctance?'

'No.' I signed my name quickly.

I told myself I'd feel easier after I'd visited the cottage a few more times. Paul bought us a beautiful flowering cherry tree and we were planting it in thigh-high rye, growing where I anticipated a smooth velvet lawn... I could see myself in wide-brimmed straw hat, Laura Ashley dress, arms full of lavender and watching someone else cut the grass... when suddenly there was a great echoing boom. Jess yelped and dived under a hedge. We blocked our ears as a jet roared over from nearby Coltishall.

It was only the first fart in cloud-cuckoo land.

On moving day one son was sick at school.

'You can't be sick outside the staff-room, boy,' roared an irate teacher. 'What have you been eating?'

'Only school dinner, sir.'

Moving is an upheaval whichever way you look at it.

We economised by using a small unknown removals firm. On a very wet day. Colin had to unhinge the front door to allow furniture to be shifted through it. While he was refixing it, the removal men shot off with a first load to Homestead. We sped after them... too late. They'd dumped all our furniture in a tangled pyramid and left.

Back home, more wet possessions were being carted out. The removals boss was wearing Colin's waterproof coat he'd snaffled, his mate trailed behind sopping and Paul, whom they'd recruited to help with the really heavy stuff, was dripping under a large leather cowboy hat.

'Anybody want fish and chips?' I stopped them in their tracks.

As we dipped into greasy paper, the boss explained how his mate's wife had to go to the dentist that afternoon.

'An' he's got to take her, a'n't he? See, we didn't know this was going to be an all-day job. Aviaries and sheds and things. Nobody never told us that. And I was going to give him a lift to collect her. What do I do now? Stop loading?'

While Colin drove the boss's mate to collect his wife, I sat in the front of the van with the last load of furniture. As we pulled away I stole a last long look at the house where my children had skipped through childhood.

I still ask myself if I would have agreed to the move had I known what lay ahead. Colin said the cottage was his patch of paradise - but then, he didn't know what was going to happen, either.

That night we both slept on armchairs amid the debris. Over the following days I developed a fetish for spraying perfume, trying to mask indescribable smells in the scullery. Then mice started scuttling around. I was on to the Council in a whisker of a second. Adonis arrived on the doorstep with a bucket of poison. I expected someone small and shrivelled. He gazed rapturously at the contents of his bucket.

'Look at that. Lovely and fresh it is.' He licked his sensuous lips.

I followed my Pied Piper everywhere. He said he had to go next to fumigate a house that had an infestation of fleas. The owners might have to vacate the place for a couple of days.

'Usually caused by pets, you know?' He stared at Jess. After that I had a fetish about de-lousing her. Then we had an infestation of wood lice in beds. But I was slowly learning not to be a sissy.

Demolition began at the cottage. It was the foulest, messiest job of all. Colin lay beside me in bed, talking about it. 'You know, I reckon there's a lot the kids and I can do ourselves.'

'Do you?'

'Sure of it,' he said, oozing confidence.

When I opened my eyes again he was staring at his fingers. He'd already done a huge amount of work at the cottage and now said, frowning: 'They'll only go into a gripped position - they look just like sausages.'

We finished up laughing but I wondered about this renovation business. Sure, we had three strapping sons - into pop music, guitars and motorbikes.

They demolished and I cooked. They returned, having choked on dust and filth, looking like china-clay workers I used to see in Cornwall.

Nightly shampoos did little to rid heads of gritty bits they were forever picking out.

Soon new rafters were placed in position to span holes left by removal of unsafe stacks. I was on pins waiting for somebody balanced up there to come crashing down.

I tackled their incredibly filthy clothes daily in ancient twin tubs which, fortunately, I had not managed to give away, let alone sell. As both halves would not fit into the scullery, I stood the washer in there, ran across into the kitchen with wet clothes, flung them into the spin-dryer, then clung to it like a lover while it jumped and shuddered across the sloping concrete floor.

The kitchen was devoid of any storage space. Tins, boxes, pots and pans were piled high on every surface. When it rained I whisked them away and replaced with buckets and bowls as water cascaded down the walls. So when Colin said, 'What sort of kitchen units do you want at the cottage?' it was like a gold oak-slatted dream. But there was still plenty of hard slog before that stage was reached.

'I always get bum jobs. I'm fed-up with doing bum jobs,' was one regular moan from the boys. But then Colin hired a trencher ready to sink cables. It was heavy and unwieldy but any mechanical aid immediately transformed bum jobs into coveted ones.

'Dad's had to go to hospital, mum,' the boys told me one day when they returned from working at the cottage.

'What?'

They'd been breaking up a lath and plaster ceiling when Colin gingerly placed his foot on it. Not gingerly enough. As it collapsed under him, he flung up his arms and grabbed the rafters for support. He left hospital with his arm encased in plaster.

'Damn cottage,' I cursed as he refused to wear the triangular bandage they'd given him.

By the end of October they had felted the roof and nailed up seven hundred feet of tiling splines. There was always someone passing something up to someone to pass to Colin as he crawled along the ridge.

Winter 1977 set in hard. Colin's enthusiasm for the place never ebbed.

But noses were red and eyes crying in the biting wind.

I was worried in case he overdid things and persuaded him to go for a medical check-up. The doctor declared his heart and blood pressure were fine. Then it was my turn. A JCB cleared brambles and tree-trunks from the front of the cottage and, anticipating a stately-home approach, I rushed out to buy sacks of daffodil bulbs. But the ground was full of hard-core. After a session of smashing it with a big hammer I woke in the night with chest pains.

'Blood pressure normal; heart pumping like mine,' said the doctor. But I'd hurt my back. Without warning he pressed his knee into it and jerked it into place. I burst into tears.

'Does it hurt?' he asked.

'No,' I sniffed.

'Haven't you moved house recently?... extremely stressful, you know. Extremely.'

I insisted no one worked at the cottage on Christmas day.

I was in the old kitchen, balloons and garlands draped between boxes and bins when I looked up and saw tiny silver flakes floating about and settling on mince-pies, cream and other festive fayre.

Colin, like me, obviously considered that crummy kitchen was best suited to be a workshop and was sitting in the corner stripping an old electric cable, releasing clouds of mica particles everywhere.

I flung open doors and windows bawling, 'I will never ever have another Christmas like this one! Never!'

How much more I could and should have valued just being together. But we don't. Until it's too late.

THREE

'Pay an extra sixty pounds to have electricity cables underground?'

We studied the big power pole at the cottage, close to where the kitchen window would be.

'Is it really in the way?' I said. 'Really so ugly?'

Finally Colin swiped through our attempts at pretence: 'It's a total eyesore.'

So we paid for extra "abnormal" costs and awaited developments.

Meanwhile Seán quit the Sixth Form. We all did our bit to persuade him to change his mind, thinking we knew better than he did, but he was adamant. He said he would help at the cottage.

A team arrived to lay underground electricity cables. They unloaded cable, a propane cylinder and a five-gallon oil drum with triple gas jet. As they connected pipe with cylinder and lit the burner, Colin waited with interest to see some new sort of cable-joining technique.

They put the kettle on.

After the break they dropped the cable into our trench leaving slack at both ends.

'We only put it in. The others connect it. The others are coming tomorrow,' they said. And left. The others did not show up that week. Colin was hopping mad.

The weather was dark grey. Droplets hung from bare branches in the mist. Where yellow rye had once rustled was now slate-coloured sludge.

At Homestead a new housing development was creeping towards us. When surveyors ran their tapes around the old house it became clear time was of the essence. Everyone caught colds and was irritable. Rain poured down inside walls. I was renewing sodden newspapers on the scullery floor when there was a plaintive nasal whine from the lavatory.

'It won't flush - the handle's broken.'

'Fix it then!' Colin jabbed the fire with the poker. The damper crashed into the hearth and soot avalanched after it.

'What's happened?' I peered round the door and knocked over a bottle of squash. Fragments of glass shot into a pudding waiting to be eaten. I toyed with the idea of leaving them in there.

I wrote in my diary: "I'm fed up with snotty noses, arguments, weather, wet washing hanging like sore fingers in the kitchen - everything! Paul spilt orange juice in the freezer. Colin and I can hardly move with back-ache... I've had ENOUGH."

Everyone worried about trenches caving in if it didn't stop raining. But it did stop and work began again. Glass replaced boards at windows.

The cottage was opening her eyes.

More groups arrived from the Electricity Board. One lot did things to the transformer on a power pole in the loke. We assumed the man who steadied the ladder was a supervisor because he had a different-coloured helmet and a proper car. The other men took turns to chop down our power-pole with a huge axe.

'This is a swine,' they gasped.

'Oh, I don't know,' quipped Colin, elated they'd turned up at all, 'you've got the branches off already.'

He didn't think it was funny for long. Two of the men held ropes so it would not fall on our shed or the tiny touring caravan we'd brought on site.

Instead it fell a whatsit's width from Colin's cottage.

Eager for power to be installed Colin plotted the position of an outside meter on the soon-to-be-built extension. He conjured up a wooden box with waterproof lid and lockable door as a temporary measure.

'That's good, dad.' The boys were impressed. The electricity men weren't. 'Sorry, sir, it doesn't have a padlock.'

Colin assured them he'd get one and they promised a meter for the following Friday. Friday was atrociously icy and they could not reach us so we had to cancel the damp-proofing team who needed power as much as we did.

Snow fell like ticker tape. We dragged sledges into fields and romped in Santa Claus land. Colin showed us tracks of hedgehogs, rabbits and foxes. This was one for the memory-box.

The icing melted and the meter-men returned to a rapturous welcome. But they refused to connect the meter. Colin had driven a piece of copper pipe in the ground to act as an earth. Not what they wanted at all.

'Just a minute.' He vanished before they could and reappeared like a magician, waving a real earthing spike. I never knew where he found it. He had a knack of coming up with the goods at the last minute.

So there was power. It was everyone's birthday at once. Wander lights swayed and sparkled provocatively, enticing everyone to work late.

I decided to learn to use a gun and join the huntin', shootin', fishin' scene. Colin stood a cocoa-tin on the fence.

'You first,' I said.

With his six-foot muscular frame steady, he splattered the tin with his twelve-bore. I didn't like the bang. He assured me the smaller twenty-bore wouldn't be so noisy so I slipped a cartridge into that and aimed.

'At least I'll be able to defend myself if anybody weird comes creeping up the loke,' I said.

'For God's sake, don't ever point it at anyone!'

That's when he suggested we buy a guard-dog. I warmed to the idea; Jess was a fickle bitch and anybody's for a couple of biscuits. We spent hours reading about different breeds: Alsatians, Rottweilers and Dobermans were all intelligent, loyal and good guards. A dog-trainer advised me to steer clear of Dobes.

'They're very strong-willed; need firm-handling.' But Dobermans were the first puppies we saw advertised.

'That's what we want.' Colin's eyes glinted as a black and tan beast leapt ferociously at the wires of its compound at a remote farmhouse we visited to view the litter. In the kitchen a ragbag of puppies savaged our ankles with teeth like pins. I immediately disregarded that stuff about choosing the boldest from any litter. Then the dam lolloped in.

'You'll be OK providing you stand still,' warned the owner raising a forefinger. Unnecessary advice. The huge black and tan bitch patrolled the room. Slowly she approached me, laid her head on my lap and gazed at me with chocolate almond eyes.

'She wants her ears tickled,' said the breeder, adding a cunning, 'she likes you.' But I already knew she was magnificent.

After long deliberation we chose Carla. As we drove home our little warrior realised she'd left the pack behind and howled pitifully. She crawled under my sweater and I cuddled her. We didn't take any notice of Colin's mumblings about guard-dogs.

Jess snarled continually at Carla so we put the puppy's basket in our bedroom. At three o'clock in the morning she kicked up all hell. We put her back in the sitting room but Jess looked as if she would do for her, so we moved Jess in with us. In the morning Carla was curled on the settee in a nest of Martin's clothes, having stripped off all the new wallpaper.

The next night she howled again. We were all exhausted. But we'd sussed out the problem. The poor little pup was cold sleeping on her own in the unheated house. The next night, pushed against a small radiator and snuggled in woollies with a hot water bottle beside her, she slept like the baby she was.

Small piddles we expected but not great puddles soaking into the carpet. Jess, who had been acting like an upstaged diva, now expected to share all privileges. The pup had to be trained as a matter of some urgency. But the world outside was Arctic and a Dobe's hair is short. We took turns in shivering in the wind persuading her to, "Hurry-up".

Jess started playing with her - fun games like corner your opponent and squeeze her against the wall until she squeals, a game that lost its attraction as Carla grew bigger and stronger. But Carla loved Jess with all her being.

'Talk to your Doberman in a deeper voice - like a German border-guard,' said the trainer at dog-obedience classes. I passed this snippet on to the rest of the family and as voices dropped several decibels Carla regarded us all as her own pack of kindly fools. But before you could bawl, 'Leave!' she became a wild and wilful adolescent.

'Our trainer says you shouldn't smack a dog,' I told Colin after Carla tore up a carpet.

'Load of old rubbish,' he said. Even so, it was Colin she slavered over and adored.

But then, most females did.

The cottage grew and prospered but we were still in the old cold house. Its drab surroundings were having a dire effect on me. I continually banked up the coal fire and slopped around wearing pyjamas under a tracksuit with football socks and an old woolly hat. When Colin produced tickets for the firm's dinner-dance, I "lost" them behind the clock. I was not searching through packing cases for a best frock. Besides I would have to have a bath and I'd seen another mouse in the bathroom.

One morning a friend arrived without warning. She looked super-smart in stylish cherry-red jacket and grey pleated skirt. Hiding behind boxes in the scullery, I realised I'd become part of the clutter. It was time to drag myself up by the thermals. There would be a wonderful trans-formation. Cinderella would go to the ball.

The future is fragile as cobwebs; I hadn't learned then to take nothing for granted. On the evening of the dance Colin staggered home in excruciating pain. For the third time in his life he had kidney stones. He'd been told his threshold of pain was very high but this was enough to make him writhe in agony all night. Neither the cottage nor the dance mattered a tuppenny-damn. Only Colin mattered.

He passed the stone a couple of days later and was advised to avoid all dairy produce and food high in oxalic acid, such as rhubarb, strawberries and tomatoes.

One morning I was alone in the house baking bread when the chimney caught fire. Crackling crimson sparks and choking black smoke belched from the pot outside. Inside walls were red-hot. I frantically cleared soot from the hearth but as more plummeted, I panicked. With no telephone in the house, I raced to the firm where Colin worked, three hundred yards away.

I shouted to the receptionist as I burst through the doors.

'Call the fire brigade quick!'

While I waited in reception, smart busy executives and elegant secretaries bustled past and glanced at me curiously. I was covered in soot and flour.

The house was not razed to the ground. And I made a point of calling at the firm again at the earliest opportunity. Looking as glamorous as two hours intense preparation could muster.

There was no end to ordering fuel that winter.

'You still here?' cackled the coalman.

Was spring ever coming?

Colin taught Martin to use the theodolite and they set out the sitting-room extension at the cottage.

'Come and look at this, duck,' Colin called to me. 'It'll be too late to change your mind once foundations are laid.'

Apparently it would be expensive to shift them. It wasn't just a case of chucking back a bit of soil - you'd need shuttering and concrete...

'You're the expert,' I conceded, looking at it dubiously.

'Oh, no. You say what you're thinking.'

'I thought it was going to be a big room?'

That's what he was waiting for, of course. He explained in his patient way, 'It's an optical illusion that rooms set out on the ground always look smaller than they're going to be. It happens all the time. I was setting out an extension at a house and the owner walked down the garden, ground in his heel and shouted, "This'll do," without realising he was going to get a room thirty-six feet wide. People only relate to other rooms.'

I glanced again at the proposed extension.

'Well, if you say so.'

He grinned. 'Believe me.'

About this time a very pregnant acquaintance of mine and her husband unaccountably drove to see the cottage. After bumping along the loke he told her she'd be safer walking. When they finally arrived he looked around knowledgeably and gave Colin the benefit of his advice.

'Personally, I'd have chopped that hedge down, old boy. Not having a breakfast-bar? I'd definitely have a breakfast-bar... Are you going to round off the corners of these sills?... Good God. I didn't know you could still use that type of lintel...'

'Honestly, I hardly know them,' I protested after they'd left.

'I don't want that prat up here again!'

On May Bank Holiday Colin enlisted the boys to help him lay water pipes along the loke to the cottage. Previous tenants had carried their water from a nearby well, but I didn't rave about that.

A neighbouring farmer, had kindly agreed to us trenching along the edge of his field, saying, 'If neighbours can't help one another then it's a poor old world.'

Colin could only hire the trencher again for the weekend and was anxious to get the job completed in this time. Not easy for those new to the art of pipe laying. After a trench was dug, he took out the first huge hundred-metre coil of polythene pipe. Each few turns were tied with small pieces of string and to save time he snipped all the pieces in one go.

Everything exploded like a massive clock-spring and three hundred feet of gigantic snake hurtled down the loke.

'Catch it!' he yelled.

They all raced after the bumping bouncing pipe and hung on for dear life. At last they managed to tie one end to the car while other spirals burst open in hedges and ditches. They were finally pinned down with logs and boulders until they could be disentangled. With a mighty effort the serpent was forced into the trench but only stopped wriggling when everybody jumped on it.

But they learned. With the next coil it was a simple matter of roll and cut, repeated.

Meanwhile I did enough cooking to assuage gargantuan appetites, devising one-pot meals on the stove of the tiny touring caravan.

On Saturday night there was mutiny among the men.

'It is supposed to be a holiday, dad!'

'OK,' said Colin. 'We'll lay off Sunday, provided we finish Monday.'

And so it was agreed. On Monday it was bucketing down. They gouged out sludgy trenches and wallowed in slime. No wetter pipes were ever laid.

Colin announced proudly that his calculations had been on the button; after laying nine hundred metres of pipe there was only one metre over at the finish. But an even greater source of pride to both of us was the way our sons worked, finally emerging from the soaking loke looking like mud wrestlers.

Then Colin hired John for a week. He considered him to be the firm's best bricklayer. John had already visited the cottage before Colin began repairing the roof. The two of them had discussed the best way of demolishing the old cracked chimney.

'You could tie it with a rope, bor, or get yourself some scaffolding…' The debate continued solemnly, only brought to a halt when John grabbed a ladder, climbed over the sliding roof tiles, wrenched off the masonry bit by bit and chucked it over the gable end. That was that sorted.

Colin took time off to be John's labourer. Most brickies prefer working with the gang they are used to. And after all, Colin worked in the office - a "soft" job. But he also spent time on site where he was very well liked, and he and John got on together. By the end of the first day they had built the sitting-room extension up to eye-level and had set in all window frames.

We followed the brickies' code and spent evenings stacking bricks ready for John to use the next morning and filled huge water drums... the water tap was halfway along the loke so it was a case of driving down there with bulky containers and heaving them into the car.

At the end of the week we had a new living area with bedroom above. After the birth of new rooms we were on a high and bought a bathroom suite. When it stood green, gleaming and unconnected in the cottage I would stand and gaze at it to remind myself life wouldn't always be muck and slog.

Colin had wanted to make full use of the rare spell of fine weather while John was with us, so he delayed concreting the sitting-room floor until the walls were built, although he knew this was the wrong way round to do it. Hardcore was blinded off (made nice and smooth with sand) as 1000 gauge polythene was to be covered with four-inch deep concrete. Then Colin made a horrible discovery.

'I can't wangle the blasted wheelbarrow round the corners of the hall to the lounge,' he moaned.

So everyone mixed, carried and poured for hours. Using buckets.

Seán and Colin completed the floor that evening, working until dark, carting in the last concrete, bucket after bucket after bucket. To use an expression of my dad's - they played a blinder.

The end of May was glorious. I listened to comforting sounds from nearby gardens around old Homestead. Suddenly I decided I liked the area... good shops and bus stops in walking distance, faces becoming familiar. And it wasn't isolated.

The time had definitely come to bite the bullet.

FOUR

There was a huge amount to be done before the cottage was anything like habitable, but as it was nice and sunny, it seemed a good time to make the permanent move into the country. I was still a bit worried about living in the middle of meadows. Perhaps sunshine and birdsong would absolve doubts.

We toured Norfolk looking for a large cheap residential caravan to site at the cottage. Trips were good fun. We stopped at roadside restaurants for egg, chips and maple-syrup pancakes. It was like being on holiday.

One site-owner was too busy to show us round a caravan we liked and gave us the key to inspect it ourselves. He wasn't daft. While we were in there it keeled over with one end hanging perilously over a deep wide ditch. Colin did an amazing balancing act, spreading his long legs across the centre of the van to balance it while the rest of us clambered to safety.

'You're ever so athletic,' I murmured in his ear afterwards. He grinned and cocked an eyebrow. 'It was nothing.'

We finally found our caravan. It was huge, shabby and cost £135.

'You couldn't buy a shed for this price,' the exuberant owner exclaimed. He pulled down a smallish double bed in the main living area and bounced on it. 'Blimey, you could do anything on this bed.'

A low-loader driver managed to manoeuvre the loke to transport the van to the cottage.

'There are hundreds of you lot renovating cottages. I'm always carting the same caravans around.'

I pampered that van with colourful fat cushions and carpet pieces until it was sunshine-bright inside. A list stuck behind the door urged us to be quiet on site after ten-thirty for the sake of other campers. It only added to my feeling this was one great big holiday. Until family and dogs tumbled into it, armed with pots, pans, television, clothes and bones. I'd stepped into the realms of fantasy thinking we were all going to squeeze in there.

It was agreed Seán and Martin would sleep in the small tourer while Paul opted to stay in the old house we were still renting where he could spend hours in the scullery with oily rags and sections of dismantled motor-bike.

I didn't reckon it was worth buying a mattress for our caravan bed. Surely it would not be long before we'd be sleeping in the cottage? So the long seats in the dining area of the van doubled as single beds.

I can now state categorically, those hard narrow buttoned mattresses didn't have a thing going for them. Not unless you liked the celibate life. We tried pushing them together on the floor but penetrating draughts put paid to that idea.

Rain deluged. For days. Wall-to-wall wellingtons lined the caravan kitchen. Outside, deep slippery mud cemented gaps between bricks, blocks, scaffolding, wheelbarrows, mixers, spades, shovels and drain-pipes.

What had happened to sunshine and birdsong?

Whilst everyone was working at the cottage: plasterer, carpenter, digger-driver... even the plumbers promised to come... it did not seem so lonely and I was forever rushing about clearing up after them, cooking and carting rubble... bum jobs, but I enjoyed the chat and banter. When the workmen drove away every afternoon and I was alone, I turned the radio to deafening.

'You know, I'll never leave you on your own here at night, don't you?' Colin said.

Well, that's not so bad, I thought. Won't be so scary in the day. But nothing had prepared me for the suffocating stillness that floated in from fields the first full day I was by myself. When I went down the loke for water, I carried on to the village to find people.

We'd driven through Stratton Strawless many times but had spoken to no one. And there were so many burning issues - like who was a good butcher in the area and who delivered milk and papers?

A cheery figure leaning over her gate told me "Ronnie" delivered milk that could be left at the end of the loke. Later, Colin nailed a box for this purpose on an old milk churn-stand where pretty tendrils of wild roses curled around it. I asked about newspaper deliveries.

'What papers do you want?' she asked.

'Well, my son wants The Telegraph.'

'You don't want them old London papers. Most folk here have the Eastern Daily Press. Tell him to get his own.'

So the EDP was left with the milk.

'But the postman comes all the way to the cottage!' I squealed when Colin came home for lunch. He immediately cut a slit in a still-boarded-up kitchen window and painted MAIL on the brickwork to give the postman a general direction in which to aim.

'Are you OK?' Colin asked me before leaving again for work.

No, I am not. I don't like this quiet and I tell you something else - I'm not going to make it as a pioneer, I felt like saying.

But then he kissed me...

I found it a generally unsettling time. Seán bought a motorbike nearly as noisy as his brother's. It amazed me that the inexperienced could jump straight on to these machines and ride off on to busy roads, with only L-plates to make other drivers wary.

Not as though Colin and I were his best examples. We borrowed a camping-trailer and began moving furniture from the rented house to the cottage. The tailboard fell off en route and we towed it for some time by its cable. When we stopped to investigate the clanking sound we found we'd shaken off the numberplate, rear and stop lights and flashing indicators.

We were always changing our minds about which form of heating to install in the cottage. There was no gas in our area and a friend who had oil said it frightened him to watch the level dropping. We finally settled on solid-fuel.

I wish I'd known then what I know now.

Even so, I still love open fires. Crackling flames remind me of intimate family groupings in childhood, when toast balanced on the end of a fork and potatoes snatched filthy from the ashes, took the place of a plastic TV tray holding snacks whisked from freezer to microwave.

Colin, being superstitious, insisted on the symbolic use of the old chimney pot from the cottage, on our newly built chimney. John began flaunching round the pot just as rain lashed down again... did it ever stop?

'Is the pot straight, June?' shouted Colin who was perched with him on the roof.

'I think so.'

'Think is no good. This is vital.'

They threw an old waterproof cape over the wet flaunching where it flapped desolately for days. At last, fine weather returned. John stood proudly up there beside it while the rest of us waited like relations at a christening, eyes heavenward. The pot was unveiled. We gasped. It was "Bootiful".

And straight, thank God.

'You let him do what?' I cried, when I discovered later that Seán had climbed on the roof in the first instant, to position the blasted pot. After all the scaffolding had been removed.

'He was all right. He enjoyed it,' Colin said.

Let's face it. They all enjoyed it.

I liked living in the caravan. It was bright and sunny in there. I've a penchant for sunny rooms. There were drawbacks, of course. The half-inch diameter pipe leading outside from the sink kept getting blocked. (You had to do nasty things with a straightened-out wire coat hanger.) This pipe led to another and the two frequently separated leaving foul-smelling pools slopping at the end of the van. One dark night when Paul went outside to adjust the TV aerial and sank into the slabby bog, no one would let him back in the caravan.

A great success was bottled gas. The tiny cooker had no thermostat but produced scores of excellent scones.

Colin once said to me, 'Do you know the worst thing I remember about living in that van? It was you whispering in the middle of the night, "Did you turn the gas-cylinder off?" '

I only remember him clambering outside naked, except for welling-tons.

I remember it well.

Bucket-and-chuckit sanitary arrangements were disgusting. Whenever the bucket needed emptying, everyone disappeared. Once, Carla spotted the contents being buried and dug up the lot. I never walked past proper lavatories in the City, even when I didn't want to go, although I did object to being the only member of my family who had to pay for the privilege. If anyone had told me the highlight of my life would be when drains were laid...

I was equally thrilled one day when a digger finished trenching, leaving us with an outside tap in the garden and a wide smile on Colin's face. No more collecting water from halfway down the loke.

We splashed about frenziedly, washing hands, feet and hair in icy water. We drank it with gusto pretending it didn't have the most revolting taste of plastic-pipe and jointing-compound.

Every morning after that the men stripped and sluiced outside. The cry went up, 'This is the life!'

I wished I'd known the secret years before when my sons would not go anywhere near soap. I wondered how long they would all continue to jog into the crisp morning air when winter came.

Suddenly we were buried alive as undergrowth rampaged. Where there had been a peppering of wild flowers peeping prettily through the mud, was now a profusion of briars, bindweed, vetch-grass, hoary ragwort, arsemart, deadly nightshade... to say nothing of nettles that grew higher than we did.

We actually took a day off. Colin, Martin and I visited the attractive market town of Aylsham a few miles away. It was carnival week and the square was full of stalls and sideshows. We threw darts, bowled, browsed and spent money. Afterwards we sat on the grass in the sunshine in front of the church. I thought of Wordsworth's words:

> *Here rest your wings when they are weary;*
> *Here lodge as in a sanctuary...*

I felt more at peace than for a long time.

When we arrived home there was a message to say Seán was in hospital. He'd fallen from his motor bike. Some of my sons' friends appeared so blasé about their motorbike accidents, as if they were a necessary part of the biking fraternity's initiation: 'Oh, David's OK - just had his pins out.'

We were so incredibly relieved Seán's accident was not worse. He'd taken a corner too quickly, hit a low bank and got flung into a field, just missing a heap of concrete blocks stacked nearby. He was lucky to emerge with only a broken collarbone and smashed-up bike. He too was very casual about the whole incident.

I wasn't. I couldn't think of anything worse than losing a precious child. To hell with the old "boys will be boys" stuff.

His shoulder was strapped into a hitch. Our cottage was a peaceful place to convalesce when the bustle and banging stopped. And it did.

'Can't do more until the plastering is finished on them walls,' said the plumber.

'I'm not coming any more. I've had enough of driving down that loke,' said the plasterer.

I stared into the lifeless lavatory and wondered if it would ever be any more than a receptacle for fag ends.

Our sunny day out in Aylsham had given us a taste for also doing nothing so we pushed off to Cromer, ate ice-creams and candy-floss, played the machines, paddled and watched the Red Arrows flying over the cliffs. While we were away the farmer's car caught fire in the loke and firemen were there in double quick time, so not everyone was defeated by it. The boys' only regret was missing the action.

Charlie turned up at the cottage. He was an elderly diminutive man who did the electrics where Colin worked.

Before he arrived, Colin marked positions for such items as power points, rocker switches and cooker-point, on a plan of the cottage. Then he left for work, leaving a plank on two trestles wedged between rubble on the uneven kitchen floor.

Charlie burst in and gazed around him.

'It's like Cromer beach in here!'

'Colin left the trestles so you could reach the high spots,' I said.

He stared at the trestles and back at me: 'Who does he think I am? Bloody Tarzan?'

He was a fine electrician. He had to be in that kitchen.

Gordon who laid our drains followed Charlie. I had to resist throwing my arms around him when he appeared.

Colin took levels and checked gradients of pipes then set up profiles, which looked like little hurdles, beside each manhole. A digger-driver used these hurdles and a traveller (a piece of wood shaped like a gallows) to dig out trenches to a predetermined depth.

Four-inch diameter drainpipes had been ordered and a whole lot of other sexy-sounding pieces, like back-inlet gullies, slow bends and flexible couplings. Gordon used special cutters on the pipes and did an air-test using his hygrometer... and I know my husband would have been shocked at this glossing-over of a very intricate and clever procedure.

Colin had a pile of cards and sent one to the District Council from time to time and a very likeable, helpful man called Harry would come and inspect the work. After Harry had seen the drains, Martin did a stalwart job of back filling.

I was not rapturous about having a septic tank. I liked my waste neatly flushed into the dark unknown, not stored in a pit slowly filling up to daffodil level. But Colin was very enthusiastic about it.

'You'll be able to drink the water that drips into that soakaway,' he assured me.

I never saw him do it.

In later years when I watched the septic tank being emptied, I gazed into its depths and was surprised there was no smell at all.

'It's workin' well. We'll leave a bit of sludge in the bottom to start 'im off again.' said the man with the big sucking tube.

'Lovely.'

I felt even better when I received the water-rates bill because it was much cheaper than being on mains-drainage.

Shortly after his last visit to us from the Council, Harry died suddenly. Colin said sadly, 'He died of a heart attack; so young too. Makes you think how we've got to make the most of every minute.'

And, still, we never imagine it will happen to us.

FIVE

Where on earth did we find a plasterer who wouldn't get fed-up with driving along our loke?

Easy. Colin did the driving. Early every morning, he collected a young guy called Neil who was hired out to us for a week by a local firm.

The first morning we kept Neil awake with cups of tea and Radio One. It didn't matter because the plasterboard the firm was supplying and he needed, didn't arrive.

The next morning he had a hangover. We fed him tablets and took him home.

But the next day he performed a miracle. I never dreamed a coat of plaster could so transform a kitchen. It looked wonderful.

'But how are we going to afford this rate of hours?' I said to Colin.

He took Neil to one side,

'How about if we negotiate a price for the rest of the cottage and you do it in your own time?'

Neil considered the proposal solemnly, 'On'y if my mate can come as well.' So along came Nick, human dynamo, shaven head, tattoos and gold earring. Master organiser and mixer. He sprinted non-stop with buckets of plaster while Neil slapped it on walls as fast as I'd ever seen him slap. They worked until exhausted renewing energy levels with Coca-Cola, fish and chips and Players No. 6.

'Cheers, mate,' Nick said as I handed him his thousandth cup of tea.

One evening, after Colin had been knee-deep in muck and rubbish, he drove them back, still wearing his ragged sweater and torn trousers with safety-pinned flies.

'Drop us at the pub, mate,' they said, and then insisted, 'Come and have a drink with us, mate.' Colin needed little encouragement and arrived home in exuberant mood asking about ear piercing.

Sometimes we were so tired, all we wanted to do was slump in front of television. This was the scene one evening when the five of us, with dogs wedged in small spaces and pots dirty on the table, sprawled in the caravan. There was a timid knock on the door.

The dogs went beserk. Jess pretended to be some sort of super-guard. Colin grabbed Carla's collar but unfortunately hers was the first face confronting our visitor through a crack in the door.

'Hello vicar!' I called, trying to sound gracious. I sprang up to greet him on his first ever visit to us and knocked over a full pint bottle. A river of milk gushed across the floor and piddled down the hop-up over his shoes. He calmly removed his trouser-clips. 'I do have a spare bottle of milk at the vicarage,' he said kindly. After squeezing him into the van as well, I realised how much I was looking forward to moving into the cottage. Two rooms... one room completed would do.

It was not only space I fancied, but thick walls, instead of tinny ones. An elderly friend... a sweet old lady, arrived after nursing her little car lovingly along the loke. She was having a cup of coffee with me when the jets zoomed over. Everything in the caravan shook. Her cup rattled like clockwork on its saucer.

'Christ, how often do they come over?' She clapped her hands over her ears... she never came again, except to comfort me at the saddest time of my life.

When the jets became even more active, I rang Coltishall air base.

'Can you speak a bit louder? There's an exercise going on,' said an indistinct voice. 'Everyone here is either in the shelters or wearing a respirator.'

'I wish I was.'

The next day I saw an airman's car parked outside a shop in Buxton. A sticker on it persuaded us that jet noise was "The price we pay for peace." Fortunately, the cottage walls proved thick enough to muffle the price we pay for peace.

Colin was ready to wage war on anything that polluted paradise. A crop-sprayer flew frighteningly low over the cottage. The boys were fascinated. The pilot must have spotted them in the garden larking around and he began an aerobatics display to rival the Red Arrows, culminating with a dangerous nose-dive over our newly unveiled chimney. This was too much for Colin. He raced outside, plonked himself on a huge heap of rubbish and aimed his twelve-bore. The pilot continued, undeterred, so Colin stormed indoors and phoned the police:

'There's a lunatic out here trying to circumcise my chimney-pot!'

The culprit was never discovered.

The only weekend none of us was within gripping distance of tools was in September when my parents invited us to their Golden Wedding Anniversary at a hotel near Derby. Oh, the ecstasy of a shell-pink bathroom with hot running water. Then, after splashing for soapy hours - melon, trout in peach brandy and duck with almonds replaced my caravan-casserole.

'Did you hear what your father said?' Colin muttered to me, later.

At one point in the festivities, a guest had remarked she was having trouble putting up a shelf in her kitchen.

'Colin will help you with that. He's handy at fixing things,' my dad had volunteered. My dad liked helping people.

Soon we were back at the cottage and Colin was stuffing insulation into the roof space, a job he loathed. He wore mask, gloves and oldest clothes. But he was lovely and clean underneath.

Sunshine streamed into the caravan. I loaded shelves with wild flowers, berries and grasses. I feel a sense of contentment when I think about that time. Colin had been urging me to start writing again. He believed deeply everyone should make full use of any creative ability and 'Blow the housework.' So I began a new serial for a woman's magazine. I was hammering on my typewriter when Colin returned from work.

'Damn good job we didn't plant expensive shrubs,' he commented.

'Why's that?'

'The cows would have flattened them.'

'What cows?'

'They've been trampling all over the place. The plumber told me. You must have seen them. Nobody can miss a herd of cattle in the garden.'

There was no way I could convince him that when my heroine was locked in the arms of her swarthy lover, not even a pack of wolves would have distracted me from my little portable.

If summer had been damp, autumn was what my sons described as "boggin". The sun was determined not to sink into oblivion without giving us the treat of a lifetime... the whole sky was alight with blood-orange flames. I'd never seen such blatant ostentation.

'Quick!' I'd scream, anxious for everyone to witness the spectacle as it dissolved into a pale pink shawl edged with apricot and purple. This is why Norfolk is so beloved by artists. Colin made a feature of these skies in his watercolours.

His greatest love of all.

The loke was swollen with blackberries. We had to pick them before October because after that they belonged to the devil. But someone got there before us. Colin glanced at the few berries rattling around our basin. 'Damn good job we aren't Hansel and Gretel,' he said.

I went to a harvest-festival service in the village (those were days before doubts). It put a new slant on country-living when the vicar announced, 'Those who wish may sing, "Some" is safely gathered in.'

These were halcyon moments among the muck and mess, times when I told myself I might learn to live in the country after all.

The weather was stifling that September. Wasps pinged caravan windows but at night the temperature plummeted and we huddled around a bottled-gas fire.

The drainage system was coming along nicely, like a big Lego set. In the meantime we walked a plank over open trenches to reach the bucket-and-chuckit. No mean feat in wellingtons on a wet day.

John and Colin would build a natural stone-faced surround to the sitting-room fireplace we'd bought, a handsome freestanding affair with brass canopy. I hadn't been so keen on its black bars.

'They're going to need black-leading. I remember doing that for my mum when I was a girl,' I said. But Colin associated it with his granny's kitchen range. Worthy of the rosiest memories. And the salesman in the shop said, anyway, they weren't like the old sort.

They were.

When we visited the stone-yard, Colin was in his element, especially when he found a fossil in some split limestone. The man who delivered eight yards of it to the cottage was as fanatical. This was not just a load of old rocks, you understand. He handled each piece like precious stone.

'Look at this. Beautiful. York stone. See how it's been split in two giving this lovely handed design. This creamy yellow is Cotswold…blue-green Westmorland, buff-coloured York…' He was in love with it all.

The facing on the chimney-breast could only be taken up two feet a day because of its weight. When it was finally completed we were delighted with the result. Colin had used the York twin stones as a lintel and a piece of triangular Westmorland as a key stone.

At last I began to think in terms of "home" with curtains and carpets. I ate and dreamed colours. I pinned a picture of the spectrum on the caravan wall: orange incited energy; green was restful and, most important, pink was the most flattering colour as a background for a woman first thing in the morning. I matched, mixed and shuffled colours with every draper in the city. As schemes became posher, colours grew paler.

'Not magnolia again,' Colin groaned.

I was well into homemaking by now and his next remark was anathema to me. 'Under ideal conditions we shouldn't move into the cottage for another nine months - let the plaster dry out slowly. People are always in too much of a hurry to move into new houses... they rush in, turn the heating on full blast, cause cracks and condensation. We aren't doing that.'

Including dogs there were seven of us living by day in that van; sluicing together under the outside tap, thumping around, watching TV, eating, arguing, breathing together.... oh, such togetherness.

Not move in for another nine months?

Ho! Ho! Ho!

SIX

It's usually dead quiet in the country between sunset and dawn, conse-
quently, any little noise woke me up. Like a body stealing through the
rye. I squinted out of the caravan window into the moonlight and saw
Martin wandering through the field in his pyjamas.

'What d'you think you're doing?' I hissed.

'There are hedgehogs everywhere. Come and look.'

I was not leaving my warm, if uncomfortable, bunk. It was a different
story when I heard a high-pitched squealing under the van.

'Colin,' I whispered, fearfully. He rolled into his rubber boots and
shone a torch outside. An army of rats was guzzling congealed fat,
which some bright spark had tipped as liquid down the sink and, as
usual, the connecting pipes had broken apart.

'Plaster drying out or not-as soon as there's a bedroom half-ready in
that cottage, I'm in there,' I declared.

I'm frightened of fast scuttling things and never more so than one
night when there were squeaks and scratchings in the storage unit

directly under where I was sleeping.

'Don't worry, they can't get out,' mumbled Colin from deep inside sleeping bag.

I kept the light on all night. I'd hung a basket of variegated ivy to disguise a hole in the framework of the double bed folded up against the wall. I saw the leaves moving.

'No, you didn't,' he argued. But the next evening when Jess began sniffing around frenziedly he tucked his trousers in his socks, picked up his shotgun and got ready to lower the bed.

From the safety of the hop-up outside, I peered through the window and watched him and Martin move in for the kill. They found an abandoned nest and a heap of mouse-droppings.

'Told you,' I said.

The following night a mouse scuttled over Seán as he lay in bed in the small van. He hit it with a book (I don't even like writing about it.) He'd got a good aim because he'd once had a holiday-job in a bakery where a scraper used for scraping dough from the floors had come in useful for cornering vermin.

He told me this after we'd all eaten cake-samples he'd brought home.

We found mice everywhere. They built nests in our rolls of stored carpet. Workmen tramped about wearing cycle-clips.

The big caravan floor started to creak and crack. We ignored it. We weren't looking for trouble. But we couldn't ignore rain beating on the roof like tom-toms. I woke to see water dripping on Colin's bed. He drew a ring around the crack on the ceiling for inspection in daylight, placed a bucket to catch drips, and squeezed his large frame into my narrow bed with me. We didn't sleep much. I didn't mind.

At that time (at least) there seemed to be moments in Colin's life when fate was with him. He was inspecting work being carried out in a church when a massive lump of masonry fell from the roof missing him by a joss stick. He stood his ground like Samson but it shook him.

'Someone's got it in for me,' he said wryly.

No one could possibly have anything in for such a good man, I thought.

Another time, he fixed an outside electricity cupboard in the small extension wall, Rawlplugged and beautifully mortared. He was really pleased with his handiwork. Then someone left a short plank leaning against it and when a digger-driver tipped a heap of soil against it, the weight pushed the plank right through the door. Colin accepted the accident with patient resignation and rang the electricity board for a replacement door.

'Terribly sorry, that model is now obsolete,' they said.

We gloomily anticipated yet another demolition job and the fitting of a whole different cupboard when the message came through that another door like ours had been found. The last one in stock.

As each job was completed we felt a deep sense of satisfaction. But that novelty soon wore off and the next stage towards moving-in-day would be impatiently awaited.

I was chipping spilt plaster from floors where it lay in putty-coloured growths when a heap of stacked furniture fell on top of me. I swore loudly. The grinning plumber poked his head round the door and wagged his finger. I felt like telling him to put it where the lavatory was and get a move on with that. But you have to be ever so nice to your plumbers.

In all fairness, he said he couldn't do any more, to the boiler at least, until Charlie had completed the electrics and Charlie couldn't do that until the electricity people had been and they couldn't come for two weeks because they had changed to computers and everyone had switched areas.

But at last, all attention was fixed on the bathroom.

'Ride down that loke on that old bike and switch the water off,' the plumber told his young mate.

His mate clanked off and returned, pale-faced.

'There's a dead rat and a toad in that hole by that tap.'

'Have you turned it off?'

'No.'

'Well, go and turn it off.' (Only he didn't say it like that).

'I want a wrench.'

I thought he said, "retch".

As he cycled off again, I knew it was countdown to flushing time.

Never was lavatory so tested. Colin told us to take it easy or the septic tank would fill up and the soak-away was not finished, but even he did his share of unnecessary flushing. I leapt up more than once from the icy bidet spray. Just testing. The next step would be hot water.

And how soon we'd be taking all these luxuries for granted.

The kitchen units we had chosen were not delivered, as promised. The plumber shrugged, 'I'm being switched to another job. Pity you can't just get hold of the sink before I go.'

We would. We would.

After a fuss, we were told the units were on their way. I waited in. They didn't come. More fuss. They arrived at last, the wrong colour and with someone else's corner-cupboard. Colin came home from work, examined the units, said there were two large cupboards missing and phoned the shop to complain about sheer incompetence. We'd keep that colour, he grumbled. We could not afford to mess about and wait any longer - but what about the missing units? The manager apologised profusely and would attend to the matter immediately. Colin slapped down the phone, walked into the lounge and saw the missing units leaning against the wall in there.

'I feel a right idiot,' he said to me. 'Didn't you see them being carried in after the others?' And he left to sort it face to face.

I was surprised when he arrived home later that evening, chuckling merrily. A colleague at work had told how he, too, had been assembling a kitchen unit.

'He took four hours to assemble one unit! Four hours! Ha ha!' He cracked up.

That evening, Paul and Seán were at City College but we were impatient to transform the kitchen so got cracking without them. I chipped plaster off the floor to give a level finish while Colin and Martin fitted the first two units. Like a dream.

Colin stretched himself, 'Nothing to it. Won't take long now, I think we'll have a break.'

We sipped coffee leisurely, admiring the already completed units. It was imperative the sink be positioned ready for plumbing the next morning before our plumber disappeared. Confident after practising on the smaller units, Colin opened its box.

We had been sent a left-handed sink-drainer with a cabinet to suit a right-handed one. He feverishly proceeded to empty every box of every piece whilst expressing his opinion of the business world in general, in graphic detail.

And so began a long juggling act.

After realising so many parts on the base units were interchangeable, he drilled, door-swapped and shelf altered, turning an ordinary cupboard unit into a sink unit. We ended up with a drawer where we did not expect one, a sink unit without its drawer and four extra screws.

It was three o'clock in the morning.

We sagged against the wall and gazed around. It would not be long before the kitchen was grease-stained and finger-marked. But at that moment it was the most beautiful, the most splendid, the most fashionable kitchen, ever.

The next day water was running from those taps.

There was so much rubbish on site and although we were careful to shift any broken glass, Carla limped to me one day, her leg pouring with blood. It needed stitches and an overnight stay with the vet.

Later when I took her to have the stitches out and lifted her on to the table, she began to shriek. I whispered to her in the silly voice I'd used during the spoiling period while the wound healed. 'Have you got a poor foot?' She immediately froze. Her ears drooped. Her eyes filled with self-pity. She stared at her foot with a doleful expression, not moving a muscle and the stitches were quickly taken out.

Life became hectic. Between supply teaching and typing, I began transferring the contents of caravan to cottage. We were living half-in and half-out of cottage and caravan.

One day, Colin brought a builder friend from work to have a look round. The man cast his professional eye over the cottage. He guffawed, 'You won't be in this bloody place by Christmas, bor, that's for sure.'

After the silly old fool left, I cast my professional eye over it. Walls were plastered but undecorated. Under the dining-room French windows was a great gap waiting for a step and, as yet, there were no window sills. But there was a door and a light bulb. This was the room nearest completion.

'Under ideal conditions, plaster should have nine months to dry out,' Colin had said.

Whoever in this world gets ideal conditions? I jammed a lump of wood under the French windows to stop furry friends scampering in. Then I went to look for the pieces of our double bed stored in the sitting room.

I was moving in.

Bor!

SEVEN

People were always leaving things on top of block cavity walls waiting for window sills. It was bad practice because objects falling into cavities could bridge gaps and cause dampness.

'You knocked it in. You get it out,' was Colin's constant cry. Hooking-out was like the cardboard fishing game I had as a child, but more difficult, because these cavities were deep and narrow with butterfly ties. I spent forever retrieving oddments.

Basic structures in the cottage were complete, but friends were cynical when they knew we had moved in:

'Ah-ha. You won't do any more renovation now... should have waited until it was all finished... seen it before... look at Graham; he moved into his place ten years ago and it's still not finished. You don't bother once you're in.'

They didn't know Colin was building a dream.

The workmen all departed, except John who helped build a porch Colin designed. Porches were invaluable at Stratton Hill where icy winds were fierce enough to bend scaffolding-poles. While they worked outside, I sorted linen in the bedroom I'd appropriated for us.

'What's that horrible smell?' somebody said.

'Something's burning!' Colin hastily covered his brickwork to stop mortar freezing and we all raced through rooms. The foul smell got stronger by the sniff. The hall began to fill with smoke.

I panicked. 'Where is it?'

'Look!' Martin pointed to the wardrobe in our new bedroom.

I had thrown my sleeping bag on top of the wardrobe but unfortunately the wall-light up there was still switched on and had set the bag on fire. Feathers stank... a vile singed-turkey smell. The wall and ceiling were hotter than my face.

Nudge-nudge, wink-wink, look what mum did. Colin didn't say anything. He didn't need to.

Remembering the previous miserable Christmas, I bought the biggest Christmas tree I could find. It stood in gaudy splendour with a fairy pressed against the ceiling, and we had a log-crackling time. Then my short story, "Rosie's Pride" was accepted for BBC Morning Story. I was on cloud nine.

But nothing lasts forever. I am still learning the hardest lesson of all - to make the most of each day as it happens. To be content with just that. Because none of us knows what lies round the next corner.

The weather turned bitterly cold with puffing snow. On New Year's Eve 1978 the partly filled trench connecting the new septic tank with the soak-away subsided and broke the effluent pipe. Paul and Colin trudged out with spades to replace it, stinking sludge slopping over wellingtons, faces pelted with hailstones.

Abraham Lincoln said: 'Most folks are about as happy as they make up their minds to be.' It comes home to me when I read my diary of the time:

January 1979: Dreary. Slate skies; patchy snow. Big treat to see few yellow streaks in sky. Tanker drivers' strike. Martin at home - no oil to heat schools.

January: Lorry-drivers' strike. Panic-buying of food. There's talk that NUPE might be next.

February: Martin walked fourteen miles to gain his Scout-badge. Lost the waterproof I lent him.

February: Writers' Circle committee meeting in Norwich. Blizzard hit me coming back. Snowflakes hypnotic against windscreen. Colin had said to phone him if I wanted him to come out and meet me. My old car getting more unreliable.

15th February: Six-foot-deep snow drifts in loke. Colin grumbles this country is never prepared for bad weather. Local Norfolk radio gave brilliant comprehensive service. Continual warning: 'Don't go out.' Seán and Martin capered through fields to the village shop where milkman left everyone's milk. They bought six eggs. Arrived home with three. Kept slipping over. They said. Colin rang work to tell them he was snowed in. They asked him if he'd be able to get in later! This evening Norwich, Great Yarmouth and Wells are cut off. Scenery around us is breathtaking.

19th February: Cheesed off. The cottage has disappeared under floating fog. Have been cut off for five days. Togetherness definitely wearing thin. I hate this place. Radio reports most roads passable. Not our loke, though. One villager phoned to ask if we're OK down here.

20th February: The men walked across fields for lifts to school and work. The absolute silence now is unnerving. Ghostly. Feel terribly isolated. Must write. Block it all out, especially the grey cheerless view. Can't wait for them all to come home tonight. I phoned a local farmer to ask about getting loke cleared.
'All my vehicles are out clearing roads for the Council,' he said.
Great.

21st February: Colin hired a tractor to clear loke. The driver had never driven it before and didn't know where to find switch for the shovel.

Shovel too small anyway so he gave up. A friend towed our car with his Land Rover across water meadows, tracks, lanes and wood yard to main road. Colin's car now left at end of the loke, so they aren't reliant on reluctant givers of lifts any more.

22nd February: Farmer's vehicles not needed by the Council now so he sent a JCB to clear loke. Didn't charge much. Thank God I can get out of this place again.

13th March: Rains came. Fields flooded. A pond appeared in the garden complete with ducks.

14th March: Colin brought home a plaque he'd had made to put over the porch. Made of grey-green Westmoreland slate with our initials carved on it.

Who could ever leave a cottage with their initials stamped on it? He knew!

So passed winter and those times I felt oh-so-sorry for myself. But miracles were starting. Skies opened to ribbons of bright blue. Fresh green shoots spiked the ground. Daffodils appeared, fair and golden like poets rave about. We planted lilac, lavender, ribes, rosemary and jasmine. And lots of fruit and Cupressus trees.

I thought about the time I'd tussled with myself as to whether or not I should live in such a quiet neglected place. I had opened the Bible randomly, looking for a "Go" or "Don't touch it with a scaffolding-pole" message... passing the buck, you might say. The first words I read, were:

> *For I the Lord thy God will hold thy right hand, saying unto thee, Fear not; I will help thee... I will make the wilderness a pool of water... I will set in the desert the fir tree, and the pine, and the box tree together: That they may see, and know, and consider, and understand together, that the hand of the Lord hath done this...*

Later, when I told Colin what I'd read, he said it was his hand that did it.

'It wouldn't have been if you'd fallen any harder through the ceiling,' I retorted.

I've thought about that passage from the Bible many times in the light of what happened later. Doggedly trying to unravel the puzzle. For days were coming when I would scream at God and ask Him if He'd been having a good laugh at my expense?

While we debated where to position the greenhouse, the mighty winds of Norfolk carried the bolted aluminium sections out of sight.

Colin made a soft-fruit garden with a section for herbs and the rest he divided into four equal sized plots to practise four-year rotation of vegetables: onions, shallots, beans, parsnips, leeks, red cabbage, globe artichokes, peas...

He added biodegradable waste from the compost heap to the soil and seven trailer loads of pig-dung.

Country living was going to be healthy.

We decided to sell the caravan. Why is it so difficult selling that great bargain? A father and son came, looking for an extra bedroom:

'That bed doesn't look very big, dad,' said the young guy.

Too true, lad, and the bunks are worse, I thought.

Next, a Headmaster escorting a group of children with learning difficulties. One boy immediately attached himself to Colin and asked eagerly, 'You got a gun?' The empty cartridge-case he took back to school became his prized possession.

They were a sunny group and we liked them a lot. Unfortunately the caravan was too wide to go through their school gates. In the end we kept it as a store.

I bought anything and everything that would grow and visited the local auction sale. After even more fruit-trees, bulbs and bushes, I graduated to furniture where men in sheepskin-coats poked their heads knowledgeably inside drawers and cupboards. Colin had said we needed something in the porch to hold wellingtons so I bid for an old toolbox. The bidding went higher and higher - but I was hooked. On the way home with it, I imagined him gasping, 'You paid what for a welly box?'

'It's a cracker,' he exclaimed, 'those hinges are superb.'

'That's what I thought.'

Much encouraged, I returned and bought a typing-chair for a pound. When I sat on it, it spun all the way to ground level because the thread the chair rotated on had stripped. I took it back and resold it for fifty pence.

Auction fever spread and Colin could not resist bidding for an ancient double-handed crosscut saw. At home he greased it, enthusing how sharp it was. But after he and Paul had used it a few times to start a woodpile, it was left hanging in the shed as a splendid example of its kind. And he bought a new chain saw.

The cottage now looked like a big Liquorice Allsort with white walls, black bitumen plinth, yellow windowsills.

'You want to change the woodwork to magnolia and black,' said the firm's decorating expert. 'Magnolia always looks classy.'

Didn't I tell him?

By now, scenery around us was decorative enough for a biscuit-box lid. And there were so many strange noises. I'd be hanging out washing and hear a baby crying - fly down the garden only to see a lamb gambolling after its mother. Fledglings rattled the eaves and twittered under tiles; owls and bats swooped at night while pheasants woke us at five a.m., in fact anything with a voice contributed to the dawn racket. To say nothing of "pop-pop" bird-scarers.

And I'd thought the country was quiet?

Game-birds are common as gun shots in Norfolk. We'd regularly stop the car in the loke to wait while crocodiles of chicks waddled behind hen-partridges into grassy banks.

Martin was telling an old man in the village how pheasants loved our globe artichokes. He drew Martin to one side:

'Askin' for it, they are bor. I got pheasants hidden all over this house - in the shed, down the garden, under the bed.' He recounted all his secrets to my youngest son.

'Yew do have a go at 'em, bor,' he said.

'Yew do leave 'em alone, bor,' I said.

The kestrel was different. Martin found it fluttering in the loke. He wrote in a school essay:

> *I tried not to startle it. Its broken wing hung limp. I eventually got it home, part of the way in a crash helmet on the back of my brother's bike and there was an immediate reaction from everyone. My father searched out an old cage that we had used for budgerigars and the kestrel was inserted. We placed a tub of water and a small quantity of meat in the cage. My mother phoned a vet whose wife told her to put the bird in a warm place about eighty-degree Fahrenheit. We were told to feed it peanut-size pieces of meat complete with fur or feathers so it could be digested easily...*

Finding something with fur or feathers was not as easy as keeping it warm. The boiler-room was ideal once we'd lit the boiler. I'd often felt like sitting in there myself. We left the bird with a pigeon-leg swinging in front of it but it wasn't keen.

Nearly ten o'clock at night and a vet said he'd look at the kestrel so we sped through Norwich with the cage on the back seat of the car. He said it would be risky to anaesthetise the bird but suggested we left it overnight. The following morning we waited anxiously to hear if it had survived.

The vet, who gave freely of his time and expertise, said he wouldn't operate because the fracture was in the same place as in an owl his wife nursed back to health, and in that case the wing mended in its own good time.

'Give it a name and talk to it using as few words as possible.'

"Casper" came home. It was a privilege to see such a splendid bird at close quarters. It was barred reddish-brown on top and rusty-coloured below. After giving Martin a few hefty bites, it began accepting food he presented with tweezers. All we had to do was keep a daily supply going.

Now, we actually encouraged vermin by scattering food around outside. Seán borrowed an air rifle and I dropped any mice he caught into the freezer. Colin was out at dawn every morning with his gun and the rest of us scraped up mangled remains from busy roads. There are so many birds killed by traffic in the summer.

I was relieved when they found an alternate food source - until I saw the turkey poults they bought from a nearby farm.

Martin's teacher asked to speak to me: 'Do you know Martin is walking around with little bodies in his blazer-pocket?' I believed her. I'd found a bird's leg in his bed. He wrote in a school essay:

> *I made up my mind when I first picked up the kestrel and stared into its dark eyes I was going to accept full responsibility for it. There have been times when food has been very hard to get, where none of us has been able to shoot anything and where we have resorted to picking dead sparrows off the road. I have had many arguments with my parents about what is best for the bird which I have regretted doing. I am at the moment having to wrestle with the greatest problem of all - whether to release it or not. If I release it, apart from the problems involved in preparing it for the wild, I am a little concerned as to whether I will ever see it again.*

By this time the majestic Casper was installed in a large outside aviary. He could flap his wings weakly, hop from a tree-stump and scramble up netting to perches. He made agonising attempts to fly. The rapid "kle kle kle" notes are sounds made by immature birds to the parent. But Casper was mute.

A photographer came from the local paper to take a picture of Martin feeding the kestrel and was reluctant to enter the aviary with Casper eyeing him.

Soon the bird was flying between perches. Martin made some jesses - short straps to go round the bird's legs - but it was ages before Casper stopped chewing them to pieces and could be carried into the garden.

Martin raised his gloved hand very slowly and gently. The bird flexed its body and stared around. Then with a shrill "kle, kle, kle" it soared into the air.

We all soared with it.

'I reckon it should have its chance of freedom,' I said.

'You just want a happy ending. All women are emotional,' replied Martin.

However, after six weeks of it flying, he placed the bird on a tree-stump and cut its jesses.

Casper soared freely into the seductive blue sky. Martin watched in horror through binoculars as another kestrel zoomed in to attack the bird invading its territory. Casper fell like a stone. Martin found his bird exhausted, wet and bedraggled. It climbed on to his hand.

After that episode, I kept my mouth shut about freeing it. We'd learned that, if the bird was to survive the wild, it had to be hacked back correctly, a process that needed much time and patience and carried out at the right time of the year. Finally Martin took it to an expert on birds of prey, so at least it would have the company of other birds until the time came for its eventual release.

I wanted to learn about country ways, so when the farm-manager began spreading stuff on fields near us, I asked him what it was.

'You needn't worry about it; it's nothing that's going to harm the environment,' he said, dismissing me, and went back to unloading.

Another time I charged out when I saw smoke pouring over the caravan. The stubble in the field next to us was alight. He smiled benignly. 'I waited until the wind was in the right direction and started in that corner so it wouldn't get out of hand.'

I constantly worried about the wildlife in there... even the mice. It's against the law to burn stubble now.

Summer madness hit us. Don't you feel different when the sun shines? To the amusement of the kids, Colin and I went jogging across the fields. Strangely, it was him who sprinted home with gusto while I limped behind, gasping.

'Easy,' he swanked while I got my breath back.

He looked as fit as I'd ever seen him look. And certainly as happy.

Blistered hands and aching bones were behind him. He was revelling in "paradise". Every minute of it. He said the cottage was his haven where he could forget the stress of work and being at everyone's beck and call. It was at the cottage he found his peace and fulfilment.

And I seek solace in that thought now.

Seasons speed past leaving us hot or cold but not always aware of the precious packages they encapsulate. Daft happy days that make us smile when we think back on them:

'Ooh, will you take my book?' someone was sure to cry when one of the boys tried to sneak off to the library with just his own books hidden under his sweater. It was inevitable he'd stagger from the cottage with a groan, loaded with stacks of overdue books from everyone else.

Or just watching television together. I remember Colin sprawled on the settee: 'Will you make a cup of tea, Mart?'

'OK - just a minute.'

And after a few moments, Colin threatening, 'I'm going to get it myself, Mart. … I'm going… I'm going now…' and very slowly rolling towards the edge of the settee, then falling on the floor on top of his spectacles, breaking off one of the arms. We all fell about as held them up. He continued to wear those glasses for days, balanced over only one ear - the next best thing to the monocle he'd always wanted.

Nutter.

EIGHT

'I've made a mistake with the sexing,' said a friend after we'd bought three pink-eyed New Zealand Whites from her. 'I'm a buck short.'

Colin talked of self-sufficiency and he'd decided to begin with rabbits. Unfortunately, neither of us could sort out orifices from protuberances (not easy with young rabbits) so we returned them for further inspection. With that sorted, he built six strong warm hutches.

One doe was put to the buck (never the other way round). We lavished much expensive food on her and she repaid us with a phantom pregnancy. We thought the other doe was playing the same trick but one day Colin felt tiny wriggling bodies in the hutch when he was cleaning it out.

'Blast. Now she'll probably eat them.' He quickly covered them with straw. Beginner's luck that they thrived.

He kept accurate records of when does were mated, the number in each litter and the breeding line. He was always neat and methodical like that at work, tidy desk, immaculate drawings. I couldn't understand why he was the opposite when it came to clothes. He loved to be casual and yet he looked stunning in a suit.

A friend and her husband, Bunny, visited us at Easter:

'Oh, Bun, come and look at these pretty little bunnies.' She turned to Colin. 'What are you going to do with them?'

I prayed he wouldn't tell her.

Buying meat from the butcher was quite different to watching it grow up. Colin said no animal destined for the pot was to be given a name. But I heard him talking to one, "Fred" and knew he was getting fond of the rabbits. Perhaps that's why that venture did not really take off. Although Colin said it was because it was too labour intensive and not economical.

'How do you fancy a duck-pond?' he said.

He'd arrived home one day with two Muscovy ducks and a massive drake in the back of the car.

'I helped a bloke with his house extension and he insisted on giving me these.'

He hired a JCB for half a day to dig the pond. It rumbled into the garden one wet, windy morning and immediately sank into mud. We spent three hours digging it out.

'Should have had it closer to that cottage where it's drier,' the driver complained. He left us with an oddly shaped cavity a third of the intended size. We all seized spades and turned it into something resembling a bombsite. We finished up with a shallow shapeless ditch with bottlenecked gullies and a trickle of water here and there between weeds.

Martin stabbed his spade between our ditch and the flooded loke running at a higher level alongside. The waterfall it produced added new dimensions. A tiny river wended around earth postules we'd designated islands when everyone was fed-up with digging silt. But soon all movement stopped. We stood in a row gazing upon a pockmarked pit full of stagnant water.

But the ducks went bananas on it! They swam, splashed, preened and paddled. Muscovey ducks are endearing, intelligent creatures, black and white with Lone-Ranger masks. The drake didn't seem to be in such good shape as the ducks with one wing trailing on the floor. He looked awfully old, incapable of mating, and showed no vitality, except when we tried to get him into the duck-house at night when he'd hiss and jab at us with his beak. The ducks also played awkward then, anchoring themselves in the middle of the pond. That's when we realised how wide it was.

'Don't need anything too fancy for housing ducks - but they must be protected from draughts, have fresh air and be snugly dry,' Colin said, having read up on the subject with his usual thoroughness.

Mating was supposed to be easier if it took place on water but the old drake never went on the pond. Actually it never did anything except eat.

Then everything changed.

It looked like rape to me. The big old drake buttoned a duck to the ground until she squawked.

The female laid fourteen eggs and began sitting. For thirty-seven days. The man who'd said we wouldn't be in the cottage by Christmas and knew everything, said, 'You can tell if an egg is fertile, bor, by putting it in a bucket of water. If it vibrates, it's fertile.'

We did. The egg began to spin. Then it came to a full stop.

'She could be sitting there forever,' Colin said, concerned, and broke the egg open. The only thing in there was a nasty smell. His eyes narrowed, 'We'll eat that blasted drake!'

The next day eight ducklings cracked their way into the coop. It was an enchanting sight and my extremely happy husband fed them on hard-boiled egg mashed with milk and breadcrumbs, progressing to chick feed.

We didn't dare let such tinies on the pond. Crows circled in hoards waiting to peck off heads. But one day we found the chicks bobbing like yellow pom-poms on the water behind mum, dipping, diving and preening in the bright sunshine. After that, Martin sat guard down there with his shotgun, revising for exams. I bet he didn't do much revision because those pretty little ducklings were fascinating. I wasted hours watching them somersaulting, swimming under water, grabbing at grasses and chasing insects. Mum's acrobatic feats became more outlandish. I suspected she was showing off rather than teaching. Bedlam set in when duck number two dared to share the pond. She was not allowed within a webbed-foot of any chick.

By the time the second duck had produced her brood, the first darling ducklings had become gawky adolescents that drowned three of the new babies by shoving their heads under water. It got even more complicated when further clutches hatched (that drake proved insatiable).

Colin hadn't expected to spend all his free-time erecting new pens. Huts and runs littered the garden. Each little family had to be given a turn on the pond, enjoying the influx of baby frogs.

'Enough is enough,' I said finally.

'OK,' he said.

But they were a snip. Six-day-old cobs for thirty pence each. To be bred for the Christmas table.

'They must be kept warm at this stage,' said Colin.

Again, they were so pretty and vulnerable. They scratched around in a glass-topped box in the kitchen under the radiator. Soon the room smelled like diarrhoea.

Once outside they grew rapidly until they rushed at Colin and drew blood whenever he took food into the run. For safety, he lowered a bucket in there. They attacked that. They'd go for anything. But they tasted wonderful - like chickens used to taste when I was a girl.

'No, not a pig!'

But he'd done a job for somebody, hadn't he, and been given a runt. He could not resist it.

'Where are we going to keep it?' I protested. Did weak little runts sleep under radiators?

'No bother. He's giving us a pig-arc as well.'

As always, it sounded simple. I had time to think while a Movement Order was being made out. Pigs were a different proposition from winged things. Pigs were dirty.

Our tiny runt was the pinkest, sweetest, cleanest piglet ever. But I hadn't expected Colin to leave my bed and crawl into the arc with it. He tucked it snugly as a baby in a nest of straw and fed it pig-meal from the end of his finger. It thrived but after five weeks the weight increase lessened.

'What you got to do is scrub 'im with warm water and washing-up liquid, bor,' said our friend.

Colin spread a large sheet of polythene in the run. He only managed to get hold of the pig when he grabbed it by its back-legs and wrestled it to the ground. After the pig was scrubbed, Colin emerged covered in pig muck and turned the hosepipe on both of them.

Pig put on weight rapidly after that.

'Just like putting compost round a tomato plant,' Colin said with satisfaction.

A standard occupation for anyone who keeps pigs is to lean over the pen and watch them knowledgeably. Colin was doing this before he went to work when his fountain pen fell out of his top pocket. The pig ran off holding it in its mouth like a cigar, finally burying it in sludge.

'I swear that Rasher had a grin on his face,' he said.

Calling his pig "Rasher" broke all the rules and made it harder when it went to be slaughtered.

'They needn't bother to slap-mark it. I'd know that pig anywhere. It's a perfect specimen.'

Neither of us felt easy about this side of self-sufficiency. And I knew by now how fond Colin became of his animals… whatever he said.

My parents had come from Derby to stay for a few days and my dad reckoned he knew how to joint a pig (he actually did). So aided and abetted by him we lay half a pig on the kitchen table. The other half went to be smoked in a place where there was a wonderful smell of salty coal-lorries, and inches of tarry substance lining the walls.

Our bacon was much cheaper to produce than buying shop-bacon and tasted far superior to any I've ever eaten.

'By God, it's good!' my dad exclaimed with his usual exuberance as we tucked in. It wasn't a delight shared by everyone. Seán's friend came for lunch. Halfway through bacon and eggs, he suddenly paled, 'This isn't

Rasher, is it?' I felt indescribably guilty... but there is also a sense of satisfaction in producing your own food. And you do know exactly what goes into it.

'Two pigs grow fatter quicker because they encourage one another,' said our friend. That's what Colin told me when he brought home two more piglets. They grew quicker all right and as sizeable pigs were forever nudging at the posts around their pen until posts and wire collapsed. One escaped just as Colin and Martin were leaving home. They raced into the field after it but every time they got close, it tore off in another direction. Colin charged back to the cottage.

'Five minutes then I'm going to shoot it!'

He finally managed to lasso its back legs then put a sling around its middle. It ran the entire length of the field towing him. At last they reached the pen, opened the gate the merest fraction and the other pig ran full-pelt down the garden.

Martin was late for college and apologised to the lecturer. ' I've been chasing pigs.'

'Don't be stupid, Sutton.'

I doubt if any of us had stomachs for the slaughtering part and we did not venture into pigs again, although there was talk of one as a pet. They are delightful creatures, clean, intelligent and great fun.

Being even partly self-sufficient calls for lots of time, good reference books and plenty of hard work. And we wasted nothing. Colin used concrete-blocks left over from the cottage and enjoyed himself building a smokehouse. Joints were soaked in a mixture of brine and brown sugar for several weeks and then smoked over oak twigs from the garden. The taste was exquisite.

'I'm going to make sausages. It sounds really good fun.' Colin set about preparations for this in his usual methodical manner.

There were two sorts of skins he could buy: sheep guts or a type of plastic inner tube. He chose the former and bought an attachment for the mincer. The pork was ground coarsely, rusk and breadcrumbs mixed well in and the whole lot put through twice. Skins were soaked in water and threaded on the mincer ready to receive the sausage meat.

I was working upstairs when I heard the cry; 'There's two and a half miles of sausage in here.'

I had never seen so many sausages in one place at any one time. Huge piles. Pink slippery edifices slapped on every worktop and table. One sausage alone would have made a meal for two.

Colin sagged against the sink. His hands hung limp at his sides, sausage-meat oozing between his fingers.

'It was fun at first,' he said dully. 'I just kept giving the skin little twists. Then all the skin was used up...' There was a wild look in his eyes... 'But the mincer still went on shitting out meat.'

We both stared at the mountains of stuff waiting for me to pack and freeze it. The most enormous sausages you ever did see.

Suddenly, we both cracked up. When Colin laughed uncontrollably, tears always coursed down his cheeks. Now neither of us could stop. We were falling about the kitchen holding our stomachs.

I'm glad we laughed because now, remembering it, I can laugh again.

I remember our pigs, Colin, and the rabbits and the cobs and the ducks. And how caring you were with everything. And most of all, my love, I remember you, with your face awash with merriment.

NINE

'Daft idea to build a nuclear-bunker. If there's a war we'll all perish,' jeered the brave.

Perhaps we were barmy to do it, but it was 1980 and the world talked of nuclear-war. Even in villages, co-ordinators of emergency plans were being nominated in case the unthinkable happened.

Stratton Strawless is only a few miles from Coltishall air base and we figured our own nuclear-shelter would give us peace of mind. We hazarded a guess our family wouldn't be one chosen to be preserved under the city roundabout, or wherever it was Norwich had its VIP nuclear bunker. For Jo Bloggs it boiled down to a do-it-yourself affair.

Colin read up on shelters. It appeared, the one that afforded most protection cost around five thousand pounds. What we had in mind was a few hundred and a pickaxe. Whatever we built would be more substantial than three cushions and a propped-up door.

There were no guidelines to follow. It seemed no one in the area had applied to build a shelter; there were no rules and no one to give permission. Colin approached the Council. They told him planning was not needed and that Building Regulations, as far as habitable dwellings were concerned, could not sensibly be applied to a nuclear bunker.

We sent off seven pounds for plans worked out by scientists and engineers at Cambridge. They stated their shelter would withstand the blast of a five-megaton bomb. I suppose if it didn't, no one was going to complain.

Colin studied the plans and read more books on nuclear defence. In one American book, a suggestion was to drive one's car into a hole in the ground, fill up the boot and engine-space with earth and then pile three feet of earth over the whole thing.

Self-made burial mound, I suppose.

You could also make your own radioactive fall-out detector using an empty Coca-Cola tin, cotton and aluminium foil.

An engineer friend calculated the distance we were from a bomb landing at Coltishall, how much blast, and the amount, size and type of steel reinforcement needed in the concrete.

'Right. The first stage is to dig a damn great hole,' said Colin.

No problem, you'd think. But it had to be above the water table, so the soggy duck-pond-end was out, not near the big oaks in the hedge, or the septic tank; near the cottage, but not too near...

'A house hit by blast will collapse in a heap of rubble as far away from the house as half its height...' quoted Colin, adding the confusing, 'normally.' We doubled that calculation, tramped round the garden arguing, and finally picked a place.

Our friend with the JCB rumbled back into the garden. 'Nobody have a garage inspection-pit this deep, bor.'

Colin and Seán, who always worked well together, lined the hole with polythene. They made a huge steel-mesh box of reinforcement to sit in the hole and this was embedded in fourteen-inch thick concrete consolidated with a vibrating poker.

After a week, internal shuttering was removed. Apart from the main entrance-door there were escape hatches to be bricked in later. Holes were left for a steel air-pipe and one to ventilate the toilet. Shuttering was installed for the roof and more concrete poured. The roof of the shelter was finished at ground level and a metre of earth piled on top.

After that, all talk of nuclear war stopped.

It was over a decade later when Paul persuaded me down the ladder to see how dry and clean it still was... our expensive wine or potato-store.

We decided Carla should have puppies.

'I'll look at her to see if she's good enough for my dog to breed with,' offered a local breeder.

A small elderly woman, she examined Carla. 'She's not bad... muzzle her in case she nips my dog.'

As mating began, Carla looked dejected.

'Hold your bitch still,' the woman ordered as I held the head-end. Colin was knotted into legs at the other. She glanced at him quickly as the crucial moment neared: 'Lift the dog's leg over... now put your arms round both legs. Hang on, man! Hang on!'

Marvellous how nature manages all on her own.

Days became hectic after Carla produced five puppies. We kept one, Tessa. She and Carla would race together like crazy horses, both adoring Jess who grew old and curled a lip at them.

All animals loved Colin and he was a soft touch.

'There's this goat... pathetic really; it's about to be destroyed...' he told me.

'Oh, yes?'

'Brought up as a children's pet, hand-reared, even housetrained. But cute little kids don't stay that way and now they can't cope with it.'

'Oh, yes?'

'Poor thing can't feed itself. They've given it to a goat-breeder but his goats keep butting it. He can't keep it any longer. The receptionist at work told him she knew someone who had a big garden...'

'Really?'

The sandy-coated Toggenburg lay with her head on my lap in the back of the car, fixing me with devil-yellow eyes. Back at the cottage we housed her temporarily in a high-sided compound. Unfortunately, as soon as we put her in there she leapt over the top like a gazelle and landed on the roof of Seán's car that he'd put up for sale.

'Who's going to believe me when I say that dent was made by a goat!' he snorted.

She moped about, not eating. I gave her a bread-roll, which she dropped and waited expectantly for me to pick up again. But then Carla pinched her green beans and after that, goat munched away at everything. She hated cold and rain and in nasty weather perched on the hop-up inside the caravan watching us from the window. On fine days Colin tethered her outside:

'She deliberately stood on my feet again,' he complained, rubbing his open-toed sandals.

Goat became seriously ill with mastitis. The vet drove from Norwich on Bank Holiday Sunday and injected penicillin. She lay motionless for days, too poorly to even raise her head when Colin took in her goat-mix. He fed her gently from the end of his finger. Painfully slowly, her strength trickled back until one wonderful morning she staggered to meet him on spindly legs like a new-born, minus one teat, but on her way to becoming the huge obstreperous beast that greeted us like Stag-at-Bay.

She butted anyone and anything in playing distance, especially dogs; pricked up her ears and stared all around whenever they gave warning barks, and defiantly refused to be led anywhere. She grew much too strong for me to handle.

'Her survival in this household depends on yours,' I wisecracked one day as Colin was having his usual tug-of-war with her, cursing and laughing at the same time.

One summer's night when we were in bed, there was a knock on the door. Colin went downstairs carrying his shotgun. Delighted by any diversion, the dogs bounded to his side barking. He opened the door, then called, 'You'd better come down here, duck.'

In the kitchen stood a breathless group of pale-faced Cub-Scouts.

The bravest had been thrust forward to announce they were on an all-night hike, had lost their way and found themselves clambering through bushes.

'And... and a monster reared up at us!'

'That Bolshie goat,' I muttered.

We put their minds at rest. Colin went over the map with them and sent them happily on their way. I could imagine tales handed down around the campfire: 'And there was this beast with jaundiced slitty eyes, breathing fire! We raced to escape it and hammered on the door of a lonely cottage. A huge bloke with a black beard and a shotgun stood in the doorway with two snarling Dobermanns...'

I still didn't like mice; I hated rats and I wasn't a bit keen on two slinky honey-coloured ferrets Martin acquired. He left instructions for their care when he went on a school-holiday to Rhum.

'Creep up to the box ever so quietly, Dad, whip the lid up fast, grab the dish before the ferrets latch on to you and push the food in.'

'I'm not putting my arm in there!'

'Course you can; or let Mum grab the ferrets before they jump out.'

There were creatures everywhere. Carla was always carrying baby hedgehogs as gently as any retriever. Apart from beautiful birds, there were squirrels, rabbits, moles, frogs, foxes, hares and deer. And Colin grew enough organic vegetables for everything that moved.

He and I went on holiday to Wales and visited the Centre for Alternate Technology at Machynlleth. We returned home inspired. Big ideas about our own windmill power. Colin was now very keen about not wasting anything. Diluted urine was good for gardens so he made a urine-container from a five-gallon oil-drum and enthroned it in the polythene tunnel where he grew tomatoes.

'Use it whenever you can. And it would help if you peed directly on to the compost-heap to help activate it,' he told everybody.

It was easier for them. Anyway, I'd just got a new green lavatory.

We'd learned such tips as onions and carrots grown in alternate rows kept carrot-fly at bay; pot-marigolds around tomato plants deterred white- fly and a piece of rhubarb stalk in the hole where cabbage was to be planted helped to avoid club-root.

There was no stopping Colin in his search for an alternative life-style. He took a course with the Institute of Herbal Medicine, gaining a distinction.

'Is your husband a white witch?' whispered a vicar who'd called to sell me tickets to a wine and cheese party.

I suppose it was because Colin got rid of a few local warts.

We had what is now an unfashionable system working between us. Colin grew stuff. I cooked it (I've never tasted anything to surpass freshly picked peas and new potatoes) and I baked interminably. He never forced his ideas on anyone, but his quiet influence was such that I took to baking bread from the best organic stone-ground flour and avoided products that used chemicals.

Living close to nature, I began to see how it had been possible previously to drift away from the natural order of things.

I needed to find friends and looked for communal activities in the village. There was only Bingo at the village-hall on Saturday evenings.

The main road divides Stratton Strawless. Our half boasted a picture-postcard church sleeping between wonky headstones and lively weeds. There was a pond and a bend where you had to drive on tiptoe to avoid files of fluffy chicks and fussy hens. Two winding lanes consummated a dangerous union outside "the shop" where special offers were pinned to a splendid beech-tree.

Then the shop was closed down.

'That wor a shame. That wor a place everabodda could meet, weren't it?' people said.

The beautiful beech tree was chopped down. Then those who presumably knew best about such things decreed the carting away of the blister-red telephone-kiosk.

It was called "progress".

That, more or less, was the heart of the village. But most of us didn't live in the heart. Most of us were scattered like chaff along loke, road or byway, in some cases where upturned cars died behind high hedges. Neither well-bred pleasantries outside church on Sunday mornings nor calls of "All the sixes, clickety-click" constituted a satisfying social life for me. And silhouettes bobbing black behind distant windows only reinforced a recurring feeling of isolation.

I discovered the Village Hall was not used during the day so I advertised to start a Keep Fit Class. Moving together breaks barriers. Most of the female population of Stratton turned up at that first meeting. Afterwards everyone was perspiring and chatty.

'We ought to have a cup of tea afterwards so we get to know one another,' they said.

'Yes, and we ought to make more use of this Hall. The Jehovah's Witnesses use it more than we do.'

'Sometimes I never see anyone all day.'

Several years later we would give a public Keep-Fit demonstration, all wearing jazzy blue leotards and navy tights.

One member went on to start a still-thriving Senior Citizen club and another began a Mother-and-Toddler group. There's real warmth in belonging. And secret excitement, too, when trouble bubbles… A feud started between the old Parish Council and a set of would-be Councillors. When elections loomed, the two groups would attend get-to-know-your-candidate meetings, sitting opposite one another in the hall, glaring. One party asked Colin to stand for the Council and he did so because he was interested in opinions and future building developments in the area.

Things hotted up. Posters were torn down or defaced, anger mounted by the minute and the Press arrived to liven the atmosphere. In a thirty-percent turnout, the old Parish Council was returned, with Colin voted Vice-Chairman.

Of course, my dad made the usual comments about the "vice" bit.

Previous Parish Council meetings had usually been held in someone's private house, 'Where it's nice and warm'. Now they were held in the hall where sworn enemies spat venom. At one point, Madam Chair was incited to cry: 'I want it recorded in the Minutes that Mr… threatened me!' But gradually, everything returned to normal. And audience participation waned.

Sadly, within a short time, five members of that Council would be dead.

I like to think that perhaps they secretly enjoyed those scuffles. We did.

During renovation, our sons had worked long and hard. I wondered how easily they would settle into the quieter rural rhythm. Soon Paul was off, touring France on a motorbike; Seán joined the TA and Martin's first words when he returned from Rhum were: 'I didn't want to come home.'

Fly away, guys. As they should. Paul, who inherited his father's artistic talent, took the monster motorbike and left for London to study Architecture. As for Seán, we thought he was happy following in Colin's size-eleven's, having opted to work for the same firm. But life was too humdrum for him. He wanted adventure. He rose at dawn to go on TA manoeuvres, was on watch until eleven, slept until two, was attacked, marched for miles, slept in frost under a ground sheet, didn't take his boots off all weekend and came home looking exhausted, insisting it had been 'Great.'

Colin seemed to approve. Perhaps it brought back memories of National Service - or even years as a Scout. My Dad was delighted of course, 'Joined the Terriers, has he? Do him a power of good.'

He would have been pleased to see how his grandson organised routines for strength and stamina, running across fields in full kit. An irate landowner spotted him pounding across her property and demanded explanations. I agree he should have asked permission, but in spite of not being enthusiastic about the TA, I found myself bristling. She'd have been glad of men like him protecting the country in wartime. Then Seán, too, left to study for a BA. Colin missed his mate and the gossip they'd shared driving together to work.

The cottage was expanding.

And as for Martin… he acquired a guitar, red hair and a feather earring. One day when I was in the Post Office in Norwich, I glanced through the window and was transfixed. Instead of studying at the City College, my youngest son was outside the Body Shop, busking. A crumpled hat full of money lay on the ground in front of him. He suddenly spotted me. Guitar and voice were slowly lowered.

Apparently busking is OK. It isn't called "begging" any more. Even the police turned a blind eye. I didn't. As I confronted Martin, an old man on a bench nearby found it all very entertaining and grinned into both sides of his cap.

'Martin Sutton?' someone at College was heard to say. 'Isn't he the one with the guitar, who's always surrounded by girls?' But when he appeared on TV and radio to prove his worth as a singer/song-writer we all rushed to listen with pride. After A-levels, bed-sit land beckoned and he left us to live on the backside of the city.

Before you could say "Sheltered Housing," Colin and I were on our own. I shuffled past empty bedrooms leaving memorabilia intact, from the pink plaster hand peeping from under the curtain, to books and games various… just in case…

Realisation dawned slowly. No more late-night taxi-service to run, or mammoth meals to prepare; no more huge piles of laundry; watching television programmes of our choice; unrestrained fun and games on the property where, whenever and however we liked.

But we missed them all terribly.

In spite of numerous mistakes we, as parents, made, we counted ourselves so very lucky to have been in on the fun, and aggro, of the growing-up part. Theirs and ours. I also felt incredibly lucky to still be living with the man I was crazy about. Who could turn me to pulp with his smile and tears when we quarrelled.

During one of his talks on painting, he turned me scarlet with pleasure by telling his Townswomen's Guild audience: 'The two best things I ever did were to rip up my old watercolours - and to marry June.'

The remark is all the more precious to me now. There are times when it has sustained me. I'm all for people saying nice things to one another. While they still can.

TEN

There was mysticism about Colin. About his feelings for earth, sky, standing stones, ley lines. Nature was his god. You knew where you were with him.

I was the one who was confused, from the time I was seven and stole a Bible from Sunday School, to when I went to Grammar School and a teacher told me Jesus Christ was her Saviour and could be mine as well. So I joined Scripture Union.

'I want to be a missionary,' I announced.

'A lot of girls do at your age, dear,' said my Mum, placidly.

I didn't want to be like a lot of girls so I dropped that idea.

But childhood indoctrination burrows deep and when I was wrestling with myself about us buying a dilapidated cottage in the country, I took my Bible Reading as a very positive sign. Or had my unconscious mind already accepted the challenge? If it had, you'd never know it, reading my diaries from those first years at the cottage.

April 1977: I don't want to go to the cottage. It's too quiet there.

October 1977: Colin and boys put up scaffolding. I cooked roast, baked cakes and swept up rubble. Feel very tired.

27th October: Moving house stinks.

30th October: Would they like any help outside? Not if I couldn't climb the ridge carrying a roll of tarpaulin. Cooked chicken and apple crumble instead.

15th December: Demolishing stinks.

31st December: Drank in the New Year together. What does next year hold? For some strange reason I keep brooding about death. At least we are all alive and well, thank God.

29th April 1978: Colin travelled to Wales in a fragile-looking single-engine plane. How would I bear it if anything happened to him? Won't think about it. Primed five windows at cottage.

29th April: Everybody arguing. I was cross Colin let Seán work at the cottage with a shocking cold. Martin and I have grot colds. Wish I'd never seen the rotten cottage.

Oh, such whingeing. But then came summer.

July 1978: A wonderful July to remember always. There is nowhere on earth like this place when the sun shines.

Days of real contentment lay in the years to come. Colin was at his happiest painting, soaking in sparkling landscapes: windmills, yachts, reeds, rivers, boats and, always, the hauntingly beautiful Norfolk skies. And, strangely, he included many churches in his sketches.

Every picture was a legacy of infinite peace.

Most paintings were sold at his exhibitions at the Assembly House in Norwich and the Castle Museum. I always felt that part of him went with every picture. I once declared if anything happened to him, I'd never sell another.

There was a talk on the radio advising that everyone should be able to help in an emergency and I joined the Red Cross.

'Why?' said my Dad.

'So she can revive me if I need it,' Colin teased. Words that are hard to write.

We both joined a Yoga class. We arrived at the initial meeting before the teacher. When two other new members joined us they handed Colin their enrolment money which he accepted with a grin. I suppose being barefoot and bearded entitles you to be mistaken for the guru.

I was writing every day with great encouragement from him. Occasionally I'd glance at cobwebs dancing in corners.

'Leave the housework. Housework doesn't matter,' he insisted. 'Get on with the writing.'

He'd read my work before I sent it to the Publisher's Editor, corrected spelling mistakes ('I keep telling you to get a word-processor') raised an eyebrow at absurdities, argued when I defended split infinitives and beamed with pride when my books were published, making a great point of telling everyone.

I grew to depend so much on his wisdom and judgement.

Seán left to teach in Greece and we missed him enormously.

Ten years flew by. In 1987 a great hurricane tore up trees by the roots, flinging them across the loke. The worst winds and gales for three hundred years were reported.

'That oak tree's leaning at one hell'uv'n angle,' Colin said, leaning out of our bedroom window that night. So we slept downstairs. The electricity went off the next day so I cooked on a tiny gas burner. Just like old times. London was blacked out and schools in Norfolk closed. We were all advised to stay indoors.

Months later another fierce storm ripped its way along low swaying telephone lines in the loke and I was struck by lightning as I talked on the phone. I was told it was lucky I'd been wearing rubber-soled shoes and insulated by the carpet. I left hospital whooping, 'I'm alive!'

If winter was wild, spring was pastoral. Carpets of lemon, white and purple crocus surrounded a gold and pink ballet of ribes and daffodils.

July bothered me as weeds buried an entire community. But autumn was the rest cure, drifting in on bronze and crimson evenings with ever-stupendous sunsets.

'Perhaps we should sell,' said Colin, suddenly and unexpectedly.

'What?'

'Release money for our old age. Find somewhere smaller.'

He said he'd been thinking about it for some time, that he was worried about me being left alone at the cottage if anything should happen to him. But why should it? He wasn't ill. As far as I was concerned this was in the realms of the unbelievable.

'If anything does happen to me, put this place up for sale and move into a hotel for a while,' he said.

I stared at him.

'What in heaven's name makes you think I'd want to go on living without you?' The conversation was unsettling and depressing.

He shook his head gravely, 'You mustn't think like that. That would be a terrible waste. You'd have to go on living. Go on writing.'

To carry on without him? It wasn't possible. Writing was not the great life force to me that painting was to him. He was my life force! He always had been since the moment I set eyes on him. The conversation frightened me. I refused to even think about it.

1989 was a daft year. We both bought the same Valentine's card. Two little bears hugging. I sent mine anonymously to his office in a pink scented envelope.

'It's from my wife,' he laughed.

'Oh, yeah?'

In spring we rented a caravan in the Peak district and woke to six inches of snow. We kept bacon in the bedroom because it was colder than the fridge and wore balaclavas and gloves in bed.

In July, on the hottest weekend of the year, we drove to Paul's wedding in the Cotswolds where he would marry Julie.

Colin was incredibly proud that Paul was on his way to qualifying as an architect... his own unfulfilled ambition. As we were leaving, he told relations, 'We'll all meet up again in Greece when Seán gets married.'

In December I played Principal Boy in a Townswomen's Guild pantomime. The leading lady, Iris, was petite and jolly and we had a lot of fun... what a damn good job neither of us knew what the future had in store for both of us.

Colin and I sat down and mapped out our lives. He'd been arriving home from work feeling stressed and tired. We decided he would retire early at sixty. Any money from paintings or writing could contribute towards the smaller pension. We might rent out a holiday caravan... all sorts of things. As long as we could get by.

In the New Year he was looking forward to his next Watercolours Exhibition. We went to Blakeney on the Norfolk coast. I took Tessa, now our only dog, for a walk along the beach while he painted. When I returned, he was sitting in the car looking very contented and smiling:

'What do you think of this one?' he asked.

He rarely put figures in his pictures. But this one showed a man sailing into the sunset, an unusual subject for him.

It was to be his last picture.

One Saturday in February he said he did not feel very well. We went along to emergency surgery together. He did not see his own doctor and a younger one said he could find nothing wrong with him. He was to take it easy over the weekend and make another appointment to see his own doctor on Monday.

We got up late on Sunday morning and sat chatting like we always did on Sundays. Made plans. He was feeling better. I cooked a turkey-lunch, which we both enjoyed. Afterwards we took Tessa for a short leisurely walk along the loke.

'I don't feel so well again,' he said when we had only gone a little way and we walked slowly back. We sat for a while watching a film. He put his feet up on the settee.

'My arms hurt,' he said, puzzled, and began rubbing them.

I rang the doctor who said he'd come out to the cottage.

'It's so damned hot.' Colin took off his pullover and undid his shirt. I loosened his belt.

'I'm going to be sick,' he said.

At this, I rushed back to the phone. The doctor said he was on his way. Had I phoned the ambulance?

They hadn't told me at First Aid that my hands would be shaking so violently I'd find it nearly impossible to steady my fingers in the old-fashioned telephone dialling holes.

'Quickly! Come quickly! I think it's a heart attack,' I pleaded.

I flew back into the lounge where Colin was sitting on the edge of the settee. As I entered the room he slowly and silently fell forward. I saw the life leave his face.

'NO!' I cried.

I raced across to him and caught him in my arms. I knew I had to get him on a firm surface to start heart massage.

I pulled him down to the floor. Felt in his throat for any obstruction. Tilted his head back. Held his nose. Breathed my breath into his mouth.

No pulse. I started heart resuscitation.

Neighbours arrived. They said I'd phoned them but I don't remember. One took over the breathing while I alternated with heart massage. The doctor came. Then the ambulance men.

They took over everything. I remember thinking, I should be doing it.

Nothing was real. Someone took me into the kitchen. Then the doctor came in and told me Colin had died of a massive heart attack.

He was fifty-eight.

It was February 25th 1990.

I rang our sons.

PART TWO

BEREAVEMENT

ELEVEN

I was once standing at the counter in a Building Society when a huge metal security screen hurtled down like a guillotine between customers and cashiers. All communication between us was severed instantly.

Colin's death was like that.

But it didn't just blast my world apart. It split me apart as well. The half I loved so intensely, the half I looked up to and respected was gone forever. And I was left alive.

Why? was always the unanswered question.

Like other bereaved, I built an impenetrable wall around myself. Small wonder most mutual friends fled.

I'm going to wake up from this nightmare, I told myself, as someone else stumbled on my legs and another's mumblings issued from my constantly dry mouth.

With their partners, our sons arrived from Buckinghamshire, Surrey and Greece.

Phoning them about their beloved father had been horrendous.

Could I have broken it to them in a different way? But there was no easy way. What had I said before I disintegrated? I don't remember.

I only remember the sound of a dreadful distant wail.

He had always been there for them, always protectively fierce of their interests. Always their friend. Martin wrote spontaneously on the card when ordering flowers for the funeral:

You still breathe in our chests,
You still stand strong in our minds
You still love in our hearts
For you are in us all.
Thank you.

They were as stunned and grief-stricken as I was. I wanted to tell them, even though they knew, how much Colin loved them all, how very proud he was of them. Instead, I became the child whose bed they sat beside until tablets zonked me out.

I really thought I was unique. I believed no one else could have ever possibly felt how I felt. In future years I was to learn differently.

'You do know you're crying for yourself, that this is self-pity?' a friend phoned to say.

'You silly old crow!' I wanted to scream.

It was easier to be angry. Reasoning was impossible. I simply could not believe Colin wouldn't be around any more. That his dark observant eyes would never again delight in shapes and colours; nor cry with laughter. I was guilt-ridden by memories of times wasted, deeds undone. Why had I wriggled away from him to finish washing-up when he crept behind me and put his arms around my waist? And what about those petty quarrels? And some not so petty. What the hell had they been about anyway?

Then there were all the if-onlys. If only he had retired early... if only... I tried to resurrect him. I smelled his clothes, wore his watch, collected hairs from his beard-trimmer. Why hadn't I cut a lock of his hair while I could? I lost a stone in weight in those first days and remembered how he'd once found a one-ounce weight and went about chuckling to everyone: 'Have you lost a little weight?'

'I've lost a little weight, now, duck,' I whispered.

I often dreamed he was alive. I'm told this can be a normal part of early grieving. I'd run to him joyfully: 'You're alive! I knew it was a mistake!'

Was he comforting me, I wondered? God wasn't.

God?

I took down the icon hanging on my wall.

Sometimes in dreams Colin looked old and ill. Continually striving for explanations and comfort, I told myself he might have been an invalid if I had revived him. You don't have to commit suicide to die. You can simply slide out of life.

Paul took much care choosing music to be played at his father's leaving. Colin had liked Vaughan Williams, Barbara Streisand, Genesis... so many. I was no good at all helping anybody do anything. I, too, felt I'd been stunned. I was eternally grateful when Julie, his wife, took over domestic arrangements.

It's supposed to help you come to terms with the reality of death if you see the body. But it wasn't Colin lying in the undertakers with alabaster face and stiff slicked hair. What would he have said about that hair? Everything was soft in there: soft-soled shoes, soft piped music; voices quiet as sobs.

I thought Paul's suggestion to put a paintbrush in his hand was a brainwave. I placed two in the pale manicured fingers. Hope they don't take them away, I thought. I could imagine Martin scolding, 'Mum! You can't always go around not trusting people!'

No, of course they wouldn't move them. But the thought was there. There weren't many other thoughts. I couldn't chat to a cold spiritless form. 'I love you,' came to mind, but he'd know that. Wherever the real "he" was. I pecked his doll-like face and ruffled his hair slightly. He wasn't mine any more.

Behind the cottage, the February sky had the audacity to perform one of its spectacular sunsets. Julie held my arm. Perhaps it's because she's a nurse she knows how to care, or perhaps it's the person she is anyway.

'Look, Mum. That's where Colin is. Up there. Not in the mortuary.'

And he surely was.

He was cremated on March 1st 1990. An icy wind raged against the day. Relatives collected in bunches (his and mine only ever met at funerals and weddings). The strange church was lined with Freemasons and colleagues from the firm.

'They usually have to draw straws to see who goes to funerals, but everybody went to Colin's,' a friend from the office said later (and a couple did stay as friends).

On the way to church memories had sprung spitefully into the big black funeral car, tormenting me.

'I don't want any vicar saying words over me when I go,' I could hear Colin saying.

OK, I thought, so you could have been buried in the garden in a paper bag. You would have liked that, wouldn't you? I know it. But I might not stay at the cottage, then how could I come and talk to you? Anyway, this service isn't just for you. It's for those who love you like crazy and want to say "Goodbye" in a way they understand ... and you did say you could refuse me nothing (that was after tempestuous times were over!)

I prayed fervently the vicar wouldn't be a nerd. He wasn't. He was a caring down-to-earth man who'd lost his own partner. Not maudlin or droning. We sang "Morning Has Broken". Paul had chosen a beautiful haunting piece of music for the end, containing gentle sounds of the countryside.

The coffin remained where it was.

It seemed very right we left him to the sound of birdsong.

Captains and Kings departed and I was alone. That's when the big search began. Never mind I'd seen a shrouded body at the mortuary and should have accepted the finality of death. Blow that.

He was everywhere. In shadows splicing the moonlit lawn, in the face that blended with mine if I stared long and hard enough in the mirror, in distorted thoughts exacerbated by emotional and physical exhaustion. Sleepless night followed sleepless night. During one of them I wrote:

"I can think of nothing more lonely than these early soul-destroying hours. Outside is a silent black landscape. Inside, the soft monotonous hum of the central heating motor. Turn on the radio: "You Always Hurt The One You Love." Switch off. Dear Christ, bring the morning."

I was scared of becoming addicted to sleeping tablets but couldn't sleep without them. Treat of the week was taking two. Later, I learned insomnia is so common in bereavement. Others told me of ways they found to cope with it:

Jean left her radio on all night for company. Rachel found if she drank one third of a glass of sherry she slept for a few hours, at least. Michael got up and did the ironing and watched television.

'Damn sight better than lying there thinking,' he said.

Betty, who needed two duvets on the bed after her partner died, kept a store of magazines beside her. 'Sometimes I'd read a bit and look at the pictures and other times I cried into them.'

Stella slept much better after she was prescribed daytime medication.

Nothing can take away the pain and heartbreak, but lying in turmoil while windmills of the mind spin ceaselessly, is hell. Everyone I spoke to said what a truly terrible episode in their lives it was, but that it did, very slowly, become less intense.

And if anyone had said that to me in the months after Colin died, I would have spat in their self-righteousness.

Familiar pets can be a comfort. Tessa had always slept downstairs but now got promoted upstairs so I could hear her outside my bedroom door on long still nights. She made me go for daily walks. I wouldn't have shifted from the place otherwise. There we'd be, her lolloping on arthritic legs along the loke and me sniffling behind her, fantasising about living close to neighbours who rushed out to usher you into their houses for tea and sympathy.

'Spring will be here soon, love. It'll be easier then,' said my sister Pat who lives in Derby and takes everyone's troubles on her shoulders. She was my lifeline on the telephone.

Living alone at the cottage for the first time scared me, especially at night, but it was something I had to conquer. In an effort to pump courage into myself I read features in newspapers about people who longed to leave the rat race and live in a place like mine.

When Colin had first died, nothing had been real. I expected to wake up from my twilight world and find it had all been a terrible dream? But those vacuous days were the anaesthetic that would wear off, leaving the raw wound.

For years we'd left doors unlocked. Now I was convinced it was only a matter of time before I was burgled and raped. Should I ring the police with my anxieties? They'd think I was a nutter. They didn't. The young police officer who filled my kitchen advised me on security.

'Highly unlikely any criminal would want to make a run for it down that loke,' he said. But he went round the cottage and advised me where I needed extra locks.

The only writing I could manage was to scribble notes in a diary, either baring my soul or getting rid of frustrations I'd never noticed when Colin was alive. That and talking were therapeutic outlets:

5th March 1990: That crafty … at … gave me change for five pounds instead of ten. Suddenly, because I'm on my own, he thinks I'm simple.

There is so much paperwork after a partner dies. I blew kisses when I found Colin had neatly filed all his past tax-forms and kept copies of everything. Also, making a will had made things simpler.

Soon I had little yellow stickers plastered everywhere - on tiles, work-tops and doors to remind me where to write and who to see, like Solicitors, Social Security, Building Society… lots of little things like changing joint names into mine etceteras. There were always lists. Interminable lists.

6th March: So many unread documents. So many half-drunk cups of coffee. Sorting through Colin's papers and touching his strong straight handwriting hurts. Put photos of him in all rooms. Then can't bear to look at them and take them away. Can't bear that either and get them out again.

Can't watch TV any more. Has it always been so trite?

7th March: Security assuming huge proportions. Tried to screw down the small back-window so no one can break in but couldn't turn the screw. Managed it eventually by hammering it first. Tied bells to the catch and scattered hazelnuts on the windowsill so I'll hear if anyone climbs in and knocks them off.

Everyone got worried about me living alone in the cottage. I was worried too, but I didn't want to stay with anyone. The cottage was my home where I could wander about all night if I wanted to. And Colin was there.

The boys were adamant I could ring them any time, day or night. I wanted to talk incessantly about Colin but didn't want to upset them. They might have felt the same. Others who have lost partners told me they felt the same way but didn't want to upset their families either. But to talk about our lost loved ones is a help and comfort and it doesn't matter a damn if it makes us all cry.

I woke in the night with panic attacks. Arm and chest pains like Colin had. It can happen, the remaining spouse feeling the same symptoms. And it's frightening when you're on your own with no one to reassure you.

I phoned the Locum. 'I'm getting these awful chest-pains, and my pulse is racing.'

'Do you want me to come out to you?' he asked, not very enthusiastically.

Of course I did. Even at two o'clock in the morning. Heart attacks happened any time, I knew that.

It seemed like forever. At last his bewildered voice on the phone:

'I'm in the middle of fields here.'

'That's all right. You're on the right track.'

He looked seventeen. He couldn't get his ECG machine to work. I thought, that's curtains for me.

I was amazed to wake up the next morning.

I had other attacks and always in the middle of the night. Now I worried about calling anyone out. So one day I saw my own doctor who gave me an ECG and blood tests. I was OK. But when I woke again with pains in the dark empty night, I was never totally convinced it was all in the mind.

Very occasionally common sense prevailed and I'd manage to fall asleep using relaxation techniques. But one night, I was very worried and unhappy and rang the Samaritans.

'Samaritans' lines should be left open for the suicidal,' my Dad said sternly.

Not so. The Samaritans are a listening ear for sad and lonely people. "The Samaritans provide confidential, emotional support for anyone in crisis, 24 hours a day, every day of the year." And the quiet calm voice on the telephone in the dead of a lonely night helped me in my crisis.

It helps to be surrounded by the familiar: rooms, garden, shops. It tells our subconscious not everything has changed. I was advised not to do anything as drastic and stressful as moving house for at least a year.

Blow that. I put the cottage up for sale.

I hated the first viewings. The cottage was Colin's baby. How was I going to answer technical questions? I babbled on about alkathene water pipe and thirteen-inch walls. After viewers left I sobbed.

When no offers were made I felt a peculiar sense of relief. A tiny voice penetrated my being confirming, yes, it was all too soon.

I didn't want anyone seeing me as weak and vulnerable so started wearing bulky shapeless sweaters and heavy jeans.

10th March: The screaming inside me is getting worse. It's always there - when I go shopping, when I talk to people. I see Colin everywhere. He walks past windows with his sexy smile, saunters into the kitchen, touches my hair, acts the fool with the dog. He has to be here.

When somebody says to you, 'I don't know if I ought to tell you this because it might upset you,' you can bet your life it will. A relative of Colin's told me she'd seen his ghost in her garden: 'Just as clearly as seeing him alive. Honestly. You wouldn't believe it.'

I was fuming. Why hadn't his ghost appeared to me? Didn't he know the hell I was going through? To see him for a second was all I asked (and that isn't true).

I know this sounds daft but that night I sat in the dark in his studio, willing him to appear. It was the early hours of the morning when I crawled wretchedly to bed. Was I was tripping into madness?

My first outing into the city after Colin's death felt weird. How could everything still look the same? How could life still carry on so normally? With an element of masochism, I forced myself to visit places we'd been together but couldn't manage the Assembly House where we'd had such fun exhibiting his paintings. Getting through any of those "firsts" hurts. But only happens once.

I am absolutely sure I shouldn't have been driving. Thank God I did not kill anyone. I drove everywhere with tears streaming, no care for myself or anyone else. In Colin's car that I was not used to driving.

16th March: So much paperwork! So many bills. I get thirty pounds discount if I pay the funeral bill in two weeks. I don't even want to think about it. Today I went to Social Security to ask about Widow's Benefit. I imagined Colin sitting beside me. It takes twelve weeks for the pension to come through. Had coffee in Jarrolds. People in there were looking at me. Did they know Colin? Did they know he was dead?

17th March: Collected Colin's ashes. How do I know they're his? At least I've got whisps of his hair (I've got to hold on to him or I won't survive.) Walked out to pavement carrying a dun-coloured plastic urn. I thought, is this it? Is this all there is? From a warm, breathing human being? Is this it?

Where do I put them? The last place you'd want to be is in a church-yard, my love. And I'll make sure you aren't. In the meantime I've left them in the sunny room where you painted. But I can't go in there.

For Christ's sake-why you?

I love my husband. I want my husband.

After that I couldn't eat or sleep and sobbed until exhausted. I imagined Colin in every room, every corner.

One night the pain of missing him became unbearable. I sat at the kitchen table with a bottle of whisky and a pile of sleeping tablets.

He was surely with me. It was in the kitchen, not so long before, when we'd sat and talked of death. Where I'd declared I wouldn't want to go on living without him.

I saw his grave handsome face. I heard him saying over again: 'But it would be such a waste... a waste!'

Was I about to add to the futility of his death? Cause my family even more distress? They'd think they hadn't done enough for me. And I loved them so dearly too.

Had Colin married a wimp who hadn't the courage to carry on for both of us? He'd done so much for me. Couldn't I do this much for him?

But where in God's name did you find that courage? I knew I desperately needed help. I scoured the telephone book and rang Cruse.

Audrey answered. Another kind calm voice. Did I want a counsellor to come out to me? But talking to her gave me enough strength to live momentarily with the grief. I would get through the weekend. I told her I'd go to a Cruse meeting on Monday.

I'd found my safety valve. For a moment. And moments are what it is all about for the bereaved. It is how we stumble through... a minute, an hour, a day at a time. Not trying to look into the future.

I put the phone down and did what I got used to doing a lot after that - I put the kettle on.

And I slept.

TWELVE

An arrow inked on a narrow flap of card with the word CRUSE on it pointed down an alleyway towards the side door of a large church. I opened the door nervously and crept along a corridor towards the sound of voices and peeped into the room. Oh, God, there was no way I could plunge into that chattering, cup chinking, we-all-know-one-another crowd. With eyes blinded I turned round and rushed away.

'June?'

It was Audrey, a small gentle woman. She walked towards me and put her arms around me. How I drowned her with tears. 'I can't go in there.'

'You don't have to,' she said.

There were several small rooms and in one of them I was introduced to an experienced counsellor I shall call "N". I found it easy to confide in someone I didn't know. She was a wonderful listener. During that first session she assured me it was OK to cry... and if folk didn't like it, then - tough! It was better than bottling up grief which could cause health problems later.

It was also a good idea not to make any big decisions for a year after a major unhappiness when we aren't thinking straight, she told me. I talked a lot and cried a lot. I would see N again the following Monday.

I have always been gregarious but it was some weeks before I could mix with others in the main room. I was totally inward looking. The thought of starting a new independent life without Colin was abhorrent.

I left Cruse that day, still very unhappy and bewildered, but now, not quite so devastatingly alone. Although there is help along the way, we have to take the first stumbling steps on the path to recovery by ourselves.

My marriage had been a proper little cosy self-contained affair. My world had revolved around family. Over the years I'd been happy to allow Colin to become my safety net, never dreaming that one day it would be snatched away, leaving me to jump without it.

I still couldn't believe he'd gone forever. I'd run my fingers over his handwriting as if, somehow, it would bring him closer:

> *When I look up there will you be*
> *When you look up there shall I be.*

He'd written the quotation in a book he gave me.

'Where?' I shouted at cottage-walls. His paintings hanging on them weren't enough. Even messages from the grave wouldn't have been enough. I wanted him physically; to hold his hand; to feel his arms around me. But tears wouldn't bring him back. Desperately, I looked elsewhere for proof he was alive. After all, I was taught Jesus was alive.

I opened my New English Bible at random. The page in front of me was 1 Corinthians 15, verse 12. And the excerpts I read that unhappy evening were as follows:

> *Now if this is what we proclaim, that Christ was raised*
> *from the dead, how can some of you say there is no resurrec-*
> *tion of the dead? ... The sun has a splendour of its own, the*
> *moon another splendour, and the stars another, for star differs*
> *from star in brightness. So it is with the resurrection of the*

dead. What is sown in the earth as a perishable thing is
raised imperishable. Sown in humiliation, it is raised in glory;
sown in weakness, it is raised in power; sown as an animal
body, it is raised as a spiritual body...

I remember feeling a sense of wonder. There was more to death than I would ever understand. But if the dead were alive, it raised more problems. How could they rest in peace knowing the great sadness their loved ones were experiencing? I recognised my own selfishness. Deep down, did I want him to share my suffering? And if not, when was I ever going to let him go?

Questions and answers pounded my head. I had to delve as far as I could, dangerous or not. I sat in the gloomy half-light casting the runes Martin had bought Colin.

'Load of rubbish,' I'd once scoffed.

But now, answers so appropriate to me popped up again and again. Cleverly written to suit most problems I imagine. Nevertheless, they were encouraging and comforting.

Unable to let go now and with nerves jangling, I drew Scrabble letters from a bag in case Colin "got through" to me. I juggled words until messages were formed. Heaven knows how many I made up...

It was like having every window and door flung open at once when my sister Pat arrived from a distant world that was becoming less and less real.

'What's the matter with that dog? She looks thin to me,' she asked.

'Course she isn't thin...'

'What do you feed her on?'

'The same as always.'

'She's skeletal.'

'I don't tell you your dogs are too fat... '

'Do you ever play with her? Dogs need to play, you know?'

If she thought I'd got the energy to race round in circles, like she did every day, tooting a whistle and swinging a sweeping brush round for her dogs to jump over, then she could think again.

She bought bendy and pully toys for Tessa. Soon Pat, Tessa and I were charging across the fields flinging or catching. The dog thought it was Christmas. She forgot all about her arthritis.

I'd decided to have a bedside phone installed to make me feel safer at night. The trouble was, I kept changing my mind about which bed to sleep in.

'Don't ask her where she wants it,' said Pat to the telecom man. 'She can't ever make her mind up. My daughter's the same. The worst scenario I can imagine is those two going shopping together.'

Then we tussled with Colin's heavy pull-start lawn mower. Neither of us could get it going.

'What d'you expect us to do with a damn great machine like this, Colin?' Pat hollered to the skies.

But she too had her flights of fancy. We slept in the big double bed together. I guess it was to keep me company. We woke at four o'clock, chatted and put on the radio. The music being played was from Kismet, the show Colin and I saw on honeymoon.

'Eh, what about that?' she whispered hoarsely. 'That's yours and Colin's tune.'

And between all the down-to-earth stuff, she listened to me. How she listened. What an awesome burden of tears and talk I laid on my little sister.

I was low after she left, but she'd pointed the way. When the weeds began their annual march towards the cottage I grabbed a rip-hook, called the dog and worked outside until dark. I hacked at hedges with shears Colin had bought with care for himself. They were to become my most used garden tool. My shears, my garden, my responsibility, my backache.

My therapy.

I was always moaning to the dog about the size of the garden. Then I visited a small local nursery nearby. The owner had died but his bright energetic little wife who was older than me had taken on the lot. I shut up after that. If she could do it…

I cleared the greenhouse and started potting and planting. Later I was to eat the first tomatoes I'd ever grown. They weren't very nice. But they were chemical-free, like Colin grew. I suppose the difference was because I didn't pee on my compost.

I never would have believed that one day I would get excited about a mail-order delivery of ladies' ratchet secateurs. Neither did I ever think I'd fritter money on seeds and plant-pots instead of perfume and clothes. It wasn't because I liked gardening either. I didn't. But if I didn't get cracking on it the entire plot would bury me.

At night, I got fed-up with hearing frightening noises (why had I never heard a vixen screaming when Colin was alive?). For peace of mind I squandered money on a burglar alarm, even though in the previous thirteen years we sometimes didn't lock doors at night.

Taking on tasks Colin had done was like learning a new language. Why the heck hadn't I bothered to take more notice of how he did things? If I had my thirty-five year old marriage all over again, I wouldn't be content with that oh-so-cosy division of jobs. Why hadn't I ever set a mousetrap or sharpened a scythe? Why hadn't Colin ever changed a nappy? Today's couples have got it sussed better than we did.

Running the home on my own made me mightily anxious. Getting to bed was a nightmare… checking plugs and switches and then re-checking: 'Off, off, off.' Then doors. Did I lock all doors? And taps. Had I turned the taps off properly? Then finally climbing into bed and listening to mice cavorting in the roof-space among accumulated junk of years.

But worse than anything was the solid-fuel boiler! When Colin had lit it, it stayed lit for months. Not with me, it didn't. With me, it died every two days. I got fed-up with laying and lighting, a process that took forever. Then I spotted Colin's earthing spike in the garden and clanked it around inside the boiler's belly. Masses of clinker had built up. Once I got rid of it, it stayed alight a few days longer.

The flickering open fire in the sitting room meant more muck and work. But it was such company - crackling and comforting - and sent me to sleep.

Like so many widowed I was on an emotional switchback. Great waves of grief swallowed me during which minor problems assumed massive proportions... like a broken pane of glass or a shifting roof-tile. It was not easy finding the trustworthy handyman who would take on small jobs. It takes time to discover where these pearls are to be found.

Or to learn to fix things yourself.

The upright vacuum-cleaner drive-belt broke. Instructions stated: "Replacing the drive-belt is very simple." I sat on the stairs forever with the cleaner balanced upside down resting against my chin.

The moment I got it working was sheer joy!

Laughter, I read, can heal and help the immune system. Even forced laughter or a pretend smile. One morning, pasty-faced and wrinkled, I leered into the mirror. Quite horrific - but even worse in the middle of the night.

When I needed to dredge up dwindling courage I'd walk round the cottage singing loudly, something like Ten Green Bottles, tunelessly, tearfully and endlessly (good job I was living in isolation). The raucous din acted like an explosion releasing a mountain of emotions. So did swearing. Swearing was very good. Very therapeutic. I didn't bottle anything up if I could help it.

Sometimes when I was feeling low I'd grasp the handle of Colin's much-used screwdriver and imagine his vibes, his strength, seeping into me.

If you believe something is helping you - it is!

I began scouring advertisements in the local paper for plumbers, builders, glaziers, and better still, sought recommendations from anyone who'd had workmen in, so I'd be ready for the next "crisis".

After Colin died I had a bad case of writer's block, but kept a diary:

29th March, 1990: Was interviewed on local radio about my new book: Mistress Of Moonhill. I imagined Colin urging me to do it. Wish I hadn't. Sheer masochism. Talked a load of nonsense. Didn't even get a cup of coffee.

30th March: I'm turning into him. Watch TV programmes because he liked them... I've messed up the video. Hate that thing. Keep staring at photos. The longing for him never ceases. When do I get to drag myself out of this void?

April: I set the video! I did it!

April: Burglar alarm is intimidating: set it, then rush off before it starts to pulsate. What shall I do if it goes off in the night anyway? And why am I so scared of everything?

Friends invited me for lunch. It would be the first time I'd been in their home without Colin. I panicked and nearly called off.

Such firsts are so sad: first Christmas, birthday, anniversary without the beloved partner. I even dreaded catching a cold without him there to say, 'I'd have it for you if I could, duck.' Strangely, though, I didn't catch one for eighteen months after he died. Did all those tears help get rid of germs?

But that horrendous "first" only has to be confronted once. So gritting the teeth and getting it over is a requirement. Subsequent anniversaries are still poignant, but time takes out some of the sting.

After I'd lied, 'I'm fine, thank you,' a hundred times, I began to think I might make it after all. But usually and without warning, when I thought I was getting on top of things, down I'd go into the pit again. So taking one step at a time started all over again.

'Just get through today,' I'd order myself. 'Tackle tomorrow, tomorrow. Accept the in and out of grief.'

Anything that keeps us going until teatime is right for us. I'd seize on inspirational sayings and stick them on kitchen doors and walls. I heard Paddy Ashdown on TV, quoting a favourite-from Appollonius:

" 'Come to the edge,' he said. I said, 'No, we are afraid.' 'Come to the edge,' he said, and they came and he pushed them, and they flew."

There are so many brave, bereaved people, but I was not one of them. My finger was continually poised over the panic button and I cried enough to fill a lake. I grabbed at any aid that would keep me afloat.

Talking was one... to anyone, to Colin, to myself. I repeated phrases like a Mantra, telling myself I mustn't waste the life I had left, life that was only a blink in the big scheme of things. I resolved to fight and not let myself be one of the statistics of those who died shortly after their partners. It kept me going. For at least half an hour.

The withdrawal symptoms from living as a pair are physically and emotionally painful. No more loving, hating, lusting, laughing... the roundabout stops. I hated my counsellor when she said I had to learn to live alone. I drove home bawling as usual and the tune on the radio was "Hold on just one more day."

'Get lost!' I snapped and switched off.

We all mourn in different ways.

Leila was guilt-ridden and sad because she remembered how, near the end, she'd wanted to strangle her beloved husband who was suffering with cancer. 'It was all I could do to keep my hands off him. But I loved him!'

John was on a hedonistic high after also caring for his partner to the point of sheer exhaustion. The freedom of release after she died sent him scurrying all over the place, never staying at home. 'Why didn't the children come to see her more?' he said, tears welling.

Peter said to me: 'I can't cry. I haven't been able to cry.'

Mary and her husband had enjoyed the same quirky sense of humour. She was tempted to plonk a "Get Well" card beside the stack of sympathy ones: 'He'd have appreciated that.'

Sally pecked at her food from a tray until, one day, she felt sick to her teeth of the messy, meagre meal in front of her and flung the lot into the garden with a ferocity that frightened her. She vowed to give herself a treat every day after that and out came the best bone china.

'You have to spoil yourself, June. It's very important.'

Many felt they'd lost status and become second-class citizens when they lost a partner.

'There are couples everywhere you look. People don't know what to say to you - or do with you. I've seen old friends deliberately walk on the other side of the road to avoid me,' said Bill.

I agreed. Then something happened that made me realise how difficult it is to confront grief. Years before, a couple had bought a Dobermann puppy from us. Now, they rang, in tears, to tell me their darling dog had died. When I saw them in a large store the following week, I actually found myself avoiding them! I could not bear to start them off crying again. If only I could relive that day. We all need a listening ear, a cup of tea with a friend. For God's sake, I knew that.

One aspect many of us had in common was the need to talk about how our partners had died. And everyone spoke of the hell of loneliness. Some found it much harder than others. Diana admitted herself to a psychiatric hospital after taking an overdose. Visiting her there, I knew I could easily have been in her place.

Stress can play havoc with us. I had lost weight, my breasts hung in loose scraggy pouches and my hair was dropping out in clumps. The body and mind are deeply affected by each other. Several of us found our arthritis worsened after bereavement

'Don't do anything you don't want to do,' said my counsellor. But I didn't know what I didn't want to do. Nor what I did want to do. I tried to listen to my inner voice. But Colin and I had spoken with the same voice. We had become one person.

Where the heck did I find the voice that was mine alone?

THIRTEEN

Anger is part of bereavement. Anger against the world. Anger against the person who has died. It's a good job I knew that or I would have thought I was going off my trolley again.

I went along to a Building Society to change our joint account into my name only. The thin pale-faced youth confronting me on the other side of the partition was unsmiling.

'Have you got your husband's death certificate?'

'Here's a copy.' I riffled through my handbag.

'Sorry, we have to have the original.'

'But everyone else has accepted copies.'

'We must have the original,' he said woodenly.

'I haven't got it.'

'Where is it?' His voice held no warmth.

I'd just had a counselling session and reckoned I was OK to venture forth without snivelling. But something snapped inside me. I didn't like this guy. I didn't like his silly stony face. I didn't care whether he was justified in asking for the original certificate. How dare he look at me in that officious way? Couldn't he see I was feeling fragile? He was too young anyway. Too inexperienced. I wasn't dealing with the likes of him.

'Give me the name and address of your head-office,' I demanded.

'I don't have it.'

'Then go and find it!' I shouted.

The long queue of bored folk behind me came to life. They craned their necks. I thought, why the hell am I standing here, humiliated, watched and waiting? I want to go home. I want my cottage.

I barged my way out. At that time there wasn't one of these clever automatic doors that glides open in a genteel manner - and it crashed shut behind me. I raced towards the car park. That's when I felt giddy. I'd had nothing to eat that morning but couldn't trust myself to go into a restaurant.

I managed to get to Norwich market and bought a bag of chips. It was a cold day and no one was sitting on the benches above the market where I sat surrounded by eager pigeons. By now I was feeling frighteningly weak and dived into the chips fast. Salty tears dropped into the greasy bag as I stuffed more chips down. Pedestrians passed by on the other side, probably dismissing me as a wino.

(As I write about this episode years later, I remember it as one of my all-time lows. Thank God there were different times coming.)

I turned on the radio as I drove home. A group sang: "All the love there was between us, hang on, hang on, hang on… ".

'I will, I will!' I ground out.

'Do you know how to change a plug?' said David after I'd had lunch again with him and his wife Trautl, friends of Colin's and mine.

'I… er…' I began.

'Well, I don't,' said Trautl.

We sat round the table to watch him take a plug to pieces.

'So - where does the brown wire go?' he asked afterwards.

'There.' We pointed.

'And this one?'

This is kids' stuff I thought and couldn't wait to have a go on my own at home. But I kept cutting into the fine strands of wire under the sheath. It took me forever and my new kettle landed up with a six-inch flex.

Wire-stripper to top of shopping list.

There were jobs I couldn't tackle, like the mower breaking. A friend said he knew someone who could help me. He brought along a man carrying a bag of rusty tools. The man examined the mower and said he needed a Philips screwdriver. I lent him Colin's. After fiddling about for ages, we all agreed it would be better for me to swop the mower for one easier to start.

'Excuse me,' I said as he was leaving, 'but you've still got my screwdriver.'

'Ooh... ahh... so I have,' he said and took it out of his pocket.

Ooh... ahh, I thought. I had to watch out for myself now!

My dog Tessa was diagnosed with bone degeneration and was put on steroid tablets, after which, she seemed much better... to my immense relief.

I still had sessions of waking in the night with erratic heartbeat and a painful knee. The doctor said the former was due to tension as I fell asleep and my knee hurt because of extra physical work I'd taken on since Colin's death. It was only at the end of the appointment I let my emotions rip.

'When Colin came to emergency surgery on the Saturday, not feeling well and his pulse regularly missing a beat, he was only advised to have an easy weekend and make an appointment with you on Monday - and then dropped dead on Sunday!'

I was furiously angry. I'd been bottling this lot up since Colin died. Now I wanted reasons.

He frowned. He explained there was no way to predict a main artery blockage. He told me of an important official in London who was coming down the steps of a building immediately after having a full medical examination and had similarly dropped dead of a heart attack.

I left the surgery, distressed. I didn't know what to believe. I drove in circles round lanes and roads. I didn't know where I was going. I only knew I hated all doctors.

But I wasn't going to make the mistake again of growing hungry and faint. I'd go in a pub... because I'd never been in one on my own, didn't mean I couldn't start.

I was the only person on my own in there. I spent the entire meal with my nose stuck in The Daily Mail. Liberation, my high-heels. It was going to take some undoing - thirty-five years of being a twosome.

The rest of the afternoon strolling through a peaceful Garden Centre was a darn sight more relaxing. I have always found it so. But finally it had to be faced. Going home. Locking the door.

The following day I joined the fragrant purple-blue world of the living. I was persuaded to help at Bluebell Day when the lovely grounds of a private house in the village were opened to the public in aid of the Church. I'd avoided being with people en-masse up to then but I found serving hundreds of cups of tea to be invigorating. That night I slept without tablets for the first time.

The respite gave me a false sense of escape from the slimy pit I regularly fell into. The next morning I was raring to go and took a photograph of Colin to be framed. But in the afternoon I felt very tired. In my case, tiredness meant an inability to cope and an unhealthy introspection. I read "A Grief Observed" by C.S. Lewis. My Colin had taken a different road to me. It would surely be cruel of me to want to bring him back to die all over again. But I was finding letting go impossible.

Fits of grief would hit me any time, anywhere. Strangely though, whenever I reached a point of not caring whether I lived or died something always knee-jerked me into blowing my nose and putting the kettle on. There used to be a vicar at my local Church in Derby, who would boom, 'Courage!' from the pulpit, only he pronounced it 'Kerridge'. It caught my dad's fruitful imagination and, at what he thought were appropriate moments, he'd raise his finger and intone, 'Kerridge' at Pat and me. We'd pull faces behind his back. Who was he to preach?

So why the heck did it work years later when I thought about that preachy 'Kerridge'?

I've never been a great little housewife but I tried to make sure I had one room that was bright and cheerful to sit in. A friend said that when her husband died it was as if the house died too. Mine only really came alive for me when the children visited. After they all came in April I didn't slump again until May:

11th May 1990: Another day to get through. Ate junk food and popped pills. Daren't look in mirrors. A monstrous rat is scoffing the hen-food. The toilet back-filled. Paid in advance at Council Offices to have the septic tank emptied and the receptionist said how sorry she was to hear of Colin's death. Drove home and mowed lawn crying. But I appreciated her telling me.

15th May: Rat man came. Said hens attract rats faster than a charge of gunpowder. Hens are definitely doomed. Three hours spent digging and planting. Don't want to write. Waste of time.

16th May: Dreamed I was queuing with Colin in a strange room. Someone introduced him to a group of people and said, 'This is the artist who painted your picture.' I told Colin the boys had each taken their favourite picture and was deliriously happy he wasn't dead after all. I was woken by a vehicle crunching gravel… the tanker brought to empty septic tank. I yelled from the window, 'You're early,' and driver shouted, 'You aren't dealing with the Corporation now, love.'

17th May: Horrendous tax form to fill in! Thank God Colin left photocopies.

Hazel from Writers' Circle turned up unexpectedly to take me to lunch. That was really nice-to come all the way down my loke. We had baked potatoes, Stilton and salad at pub and then visited Blickling Hall. How peaceful, how timeless in there. Sooner or later we all get to push up daisies. I've got to make the most of every day for both Colin and me. Before Ian Gow, the MP, was killed he was reported as saying, 'We don't know how long we've got. So we've just got to get on with it.' I'm going to stop all this crying. Can't bear to think of Colin being so distressed if I'd died instead. Is there an element of guilt in the thought of not grieving, I wonder?

18th May: Wondering about putting advert in paper - widow would like to join others for pub-lunches.

19th May: Tried to resell Colin's large unused sheets of mounting board. That miserable old framer in… says he'll give me £1 each for them. Greedy slug sells them at three times the price. Instead I rang Priory Mouldings at Beccles where Colin bought them and owner said he'd buy them back at the price Colin paid. He'll also buy any unused framing. A man worth his weight in works of art.

About this time Colin's usual invitation arrived to exhibit pictures at the Norfolk Show. I rang to tell them he'd died but, 'Could I still exhibit his pictures for him?'

'Oh, I don't think so. It states in the blurb that it's for living artists… although we might get away with it this time. I'll speak to a steward,' said a woman official.

'I haven't fully made up my mind, but I wanted to check the position with you first,' I said.

'Well, please let me know soon; we've got a waiting list.'

'So has God!' I slapped down the phone.

I easily lost my cool. I even snapped at my beloved sister after she watched children on Telethon and rang to tell me I ought to count my blessings.

I got anxious about everything. I was going mad with all the paper-work there was to do and rang the Probate Office. A lovely pleasant woman told me to write to the Income Tax Officer and say everything was in joint names. She said it was probably not necessary to get a grant of representation and to ask that any tax-rebate be refunded to me. She never knew what a calming influence her voice had on me.

I behaved weirdly. I pored over lists of deaths in the local paper, and was constantly talking to Colin. When he was alive and I was indecisive or worried, he'd joke, 'What would Colin have said?' Now I listened inside me continually for his voice, taking every strange or unusual happening to be a message from him. It cost me thirty pounds to have one of his pictures framed and the same night I found exactly thirty pounds in his trouser pocket.

I left lights, radio and television on in every room to drown the silence, and survived on Horlicks and yoghurt. Letters of condolence were put away until I found "Kerridge" to re-read them properly. But there was a wonderful letter from my niece that gave me great comfort:

> *Dear Auntie June,*
>
> *I wish there was something I could do to help take away your pain, but of course there is not.*
>
> *I know that you will find a great deal of love and support from your family, but the healing must come from within yourself, and these things I wish for you:*
>
> *I wish you great strength to see you through the darkest times;*
>
> *I wish you a very quick acceptance of the truth-that nothing and no one could have altered the inevitable;*
>
> *Most of all I wish you peace of mind in knowing that you gave him the only thing he really needed from you - your love, as much as you had for as long as you could. You could not have given him a greater gift...*

I pinned it up in the kitchen together with any sayings I could latch on to when life felt unbearable. The newly widowed have many fears and niggles. Sylvia, a childless widow remarked, 'I felt like a second-class citizen when he was alive and we didn't have children, and I feel just as second-class now he is dead. This damn country is only geared up for pairs.'

We can be tormented in many ways. Penny, whose husband committed suicide said, 'I know he's in heaven but what worries me is how I'm going to find him among all those other souls.'

Tessa was now in great pain. I took her to the vet's where she was put to sleep.

'Do you want to stay with her?' the vet asked.

I would stay. She was my dog, Colin's and mine.

'Are you all right dear?' asked a woman as I stumbled into the car park afterwards.

'My dog's dead.' The tears weren't only for Tessa. And hadn't I vowed not to sob like that, again? Some hopes!

For the first time ever there was only me breathing in the cottage.

Knocked out by sleeping tablets I heard my voice distantly: 'God help me. I'm at rock-bottom.'

FOURTEEN

'A Rottweiler? Are you joking?' I said.

'They're marvellous animals. The bitches especially are so loving. Honestly. You see.'

I was open to all suggestions when a friend offered to take me along to Rottweiler Rescue. The prowling black bears were kennelled in a field.

'Pussies, that's what they are,' said the man in charge. I thought, he must know. Six of his own were savaging his garden gate. I crept after him into the field. He gazed around, 'Now... who shall we let out?'

There was no doubt about it; she was a beautiful bitch. Her big problem was an aversion to other dogs; she'd left a canine tooth stuck in one.

'Let June walk her round on the lead to see if she can manage her.'

The Rescue man said, 'She'll get a better idea if I let my dogs loose on the other side of the hedge.'

I wasn't keen.

The massive bitch snuffled me. We strolled together around the field like good mates. No problem after all. She'd be OK for me; she was gentle, but big enough to deter burglars.

She changed out of recognition in a moment. Hearing other Rottweilers barking beyond the hedge, she charged, dragging me behind her on the lead. I left her pounding privet and told the man I'd think about it.

I knew it was a mistake to do anything in a hurry, especially in my state of mind, but even if the still small voice of calm had been within warning distance I doubt I'd have listened.

The last two Dobermans from a large litter of brown Dobes were advertised that night in the local paper. The dam had been a rescue-Dobe and there was no pedigree. I didn't care. I just wanted a companion. I handed over fifty pounds.

She was lively. Very lively. I followed her all night with mop and bucket. She woke at five every morning ravaging the cottage.

I called her Tamba.

4th June 1990: Tamba greets me with enormous excitement and wees every time I appear. And if I don't shove something in her mouth quickly she bites me with little razor teeth. She ought to be constrained when I take her in the car. A firm somewhere in the depths of Norfolk makes dog-cages to fit in cars… wish I'd driven longer distances when Colin was alive instead of sitting beside him like a turnip.

I took the plunge and decided to drive further than to Norwich and back. Before leaving to find the dog-cage place, I peered under the bonnet of the car, as Colin would have done.

'A car doesn't run itself you know. It's a good idea to give it oil and water occasionally,' he'd say.

It sounds crazy now, but my heart pounded as I drove along strange roads. I wondered for a long time if I was potty to be so nervous, but then S. told me she cried when she had to tax the family car after she was widowed. She did not know what to do. In the years that followed she became so much stronger and more efficient. And J. rang to ask me how she inflated her tyres.

I was surprised I could read the road map so well. When Colin had asked me to read one when he was driving we invariably ended up arguing. But euphoria at discovering I was capable of driving to the edge of the county didn't last long (would you believe?). To start with, a cage capable of holding a grown Dobermann would not fit into the Orion. Feeling tired, I called in a country-pub for lunch, empty except for a few locals who gawped at me.

I left my jacket potato mashed-up, messed-about and uneaten.

Back in the car I became unaccountably disorientated. The reversed road map meant nothing. It was like God had plonked me down alone on empty wasteland saying, 'OK, now find your own way.'

'Great! Thanks!' I switched on the car-radio. Helen Reddy was singing, "You make it easy; it'll be easier every time."

8th June: Damned video gone wrong again. Cost a bomb. I scribbled down everything the engineer did. Can't afford him every time.

9th June: Fan-heater broke. De-fluffed it and plugged it in again. IT WORKED! Had to touch it to make sure it wasn't live. Nobody ever comes down this rotten loke. Bill from vet: £19 to put Tessa to sleep and dispose of body. (Tamba doesn't take her place.)

10th June: Video messed up again. Tried everything engineer did. It's a useless piece of equipment. I hate Sundays. Walked Tamba by river at Coltishall. People stopped to talk to me - said she was a lovely copper colour. Good not to be alone. Remember when Colin had his Hernia operation and later we sat outside The Rising Sun and he fell asleep against the white wall in the sunshine. It was very peaceful. Will death be like that?

I took Tamba there most afternoons in the summer. First we'd walk along the bank with me peering into Grockles' (holidaymakers) house-boats. One day we paddled and a swan chased us on to the bank. Sunbathers fell about laughing. After the walk I'd tie Tamba to my chair, buy a coffee from the pub and sit outside watching people and ducks.

It was a continuation of the long slow healing process. But in those days I did not believe I would get through.

16th June: Am going right down the pan. Can't make up my mind about anything. Do I sell up? Do I stay in the cottage? Where would I go? I don't belong anywhere.

17th June: I'm not going to think about anything, especially the future. Today is all I can manage.

Sometimes, when I was very low, something nice would happen. And so it was Martin and his girlfriend exploded into the cottage. They did me no end of good. There was a lot of understanding among bursts of laughter, loud music and larking with the dog. They encouraged me to go to Writers' Circle garden party. I had not been back to the Circle or any other society since Colin died. I wrote: "It was good to be back among friends again and a garden-party is best because you can hide behind a tree." But I didn't need to do that... everyone was brilliant.

It doesn't matter where you live, cottage, house or mansion, when you shut the door and are alone again.

Cruse on a Monday morning was a lifesaver.

'Doesn't it depress you, being with all those unhappy people?' I was asked.

But many were smiling and chatty - however they felt. Of course there were grieving people who desperately needed to talk with others who understood what they were about - but there were also those who'd moved further along the road and were pleased to socialise and go for a pub lunch afterwards (it's great not to eat alone). It was wonderfully supportive for those of us who had become isolated through bereavement.

Everyone reacts differently to loss. There's no "right" way to mourn just as there is no "right" way or time to die. Not everyone wants to rush out and buy a puppy.

'I don't want a dog,' said A. who had looked after his sick wife for many years. 'I want total freedom. I've even cancelled the milk and papers.'

S. said she had prayed for someone to love; she met a man at Cruse and they married. I wonder if it cured her of her early morning wanderings. Zillions of us hit the teapot before dawn!

I was told it wasn't wise to rush into an immediate relationship after a partner dies but I couldn't imagine ever wanting to do so.

15th June: Weather dreadful. Howled all the way along the loke. Don't sodding care if I'm feeling sorry for myself. Is it just my imagination I feel Colin is still close to me? You can't live with someone, love someone for years and then be split asunder, thoughts and all. I feel his beard and his thick brown hair; his arms around me; his wide hands callused from gardening, his sculptured lips. If I don't, he will disappear forever. If I were senile or unconscious I could sink into oblivion... no more hurt. What is it like, the last breath? Going on that journey alone?

I don't believe I will never see him again.

I look back on that nightmarish journey through the first years after Colin died and see how again and again, when I was at rock-bottom, a hand was offered to me and instinct, or self-preservation, made me take it.

A friend suggested I take Tamba to evening dog-training classes.

Up came all the doubts. I was scared of driving along the loke in the dark. Oh, sure, a widow friend said she never ever refused any invitation to go anywhere - but then she lived under lamp posts. Besides I hadn't got the energy. All I wanted to do at night was slump in front of the television, whatever rubbish was on. But the thought pounded that this would be different. I wouldn't have to put on a brave face in front of people who had known Colin. This would be dealing with strangers and, more important, animals.

But what about that loke?

'Who do you think is going to crouch in the cold waiting for you to drive along there and knock him over?' I remembered Colin saying. So I dismissed the thought of a ghastly figure looming in the mist, waving a yellow lantern.

Those doggy people were among the nicest I had ever met. Outgoing and immensely friendly. Although Tamba wore me out, quite hysterical

because she had canine companions, I found the evening most therapeutic. It was all so different. After Tamba and I did our stint, I would
sip coffee and watch other dog owners wrestle, or swan about, with their
pets. I listened to enthusiastic talk about dogs, dogs and dogs. And if
that isn't guaranteed to obliterate other thoughts for a while, tell me.

Returning to the empty cottage had its usual lowering effect. No one
to say, 'What happened? What d'you do?' No one to bounce ideas off.

Dog training became my evening out. I'd postpone the homecoming
after class by driving to MacDonald's and sitting in the car with Tamba,
watching cars on the ring road. Both of us eating chips and hot apple-
pie.

25th June, Monday: 4 months since Colin died. Sun shone today. Got
the name of a handyman and plumber at Cruse. Suggested it would be
a good idea to collect names of trusted tradesmen from members. In
afternoon walked by river at Coltishall. Evening sunset from the cottage
windows was so paintable. I cried. Felt a cold nose press into my hand.
Tamba stood there with a paper-hanky in her mouth. So funny!

Isolation had its points. I could yell loudly, disturbing no one.
Nothing festered inside me. On the other hand, I needed people.
However spectacular the countryside, wide-open spaces weren't the
answer.

Why can't we have our cake and eat it?

Some people find it helps if they make a celebration of their loved
one's birthday or special anniversary. I buy brandy on Colin's birthday
and drink to him. On Valentine's Day it's an azalea, the last gift he
bought me. I try to remember the laughter and the quarrels in an effort
to alleviate some of the pain, but bad memories are slippery to seize. I
know one thing for sure. He'd be grinning stylishly at the thought of
being perched on a pedestal.

Guilt is self-torture. It creeps up on us after a deep loss, with its
abortive "ifs" ... if I'd persuaded Colin to retire early, might he have
lived to drink coffee with me in Asda at ten o'clock in the morning? If
this? If that?

Sara felt guilty because she'd denied her sick husband certain foods he liked but wasn't supposed to eat.

'So what?' she said after he died. 'He should have enjoyed what he wanted in his last months.'

Peter said, 'I feel bad now because I watch the TV programmes she hated.'

But the deepest guilt for me haunts my silent nights. Did I do resuscitation techniques as well as I possibly could? I believe so... but I didn't bring him back, did I?

'You did your best, gel; you had a go,' my dad said.

Bugger that, I think. This was my husband's life. It needed more than a "go". A mental video of me breathing my life into him and then pressing my hands on his chest plays relentlessly in my head, even though I know such thoughts are negative, especially at three o'clock in the morning.

I heard the late Michael Bentine, comedian and great television personality, say so many people need help in this life it isn't good trying to concentrate on one person who has left it. We must try and be positive. When he thought of his children who died, he smiled. He thanked God for every second he had with them and enjoyed communication with them and if it was self-delusion it didn't matter a damn.

And I found such words inspirational.

When I wrote to ask him if I might quote him, he contacted me immediately with his usual infectious enthusiasm. He said he understood about those hours from midnight to dusk, that they were hours when our adrenaline levels were at their lowest.

I babbled on about Colin dying.

'Colin did what?' he said.

'Colin died.'

'He didn't die. He was promoted. When my father used to see a funeral, he would raise his hat and say, "Well done on your promotion." '

26th June: Last night I dreamed vividly again. Colin wanted to paint and I thought, oh, blimey, I've given away his easel. Then I realised with immense joy he was alive. As usual, I rushed at him. 'You're alive!'

The next morning, Martin rang: 'I had a really nice dream about dad - but it pissed me off all day.' Paul rang and said he'd dreamed Colin was alive. A few days later, I received a letter from Seán to say he'd had a great dream about his dad.

We had a useful discussion at Cruse where people exchanged experiences. One woman said she continually had dreadful nightmares about her husband's death. Another member said medication such as tranquillisers might enhance these. It was suggested the woman went to talk to her doctor.

'Well I hope her doctor isn't the same as mine; my doctor never has time to listen to you,' said Jean.

28th June: Damned video cassette flap blowing in and out like a naughty tongue. I said to repair man, 'You told me it's guaranteed for three months after repairs.' He said, 'Only for the parts we put in, dear.' Big con.

I met eighty year old Maggie, a widow (hate that word). So spunky and lively she was. So positive. She was not afraid to tackle anything. I felt a wimp for being afraid of spending the next winter alone at the cottage. Time for some positive thinking (it's ever so easy to write the words.)

18th July: I've made a decision! About where to put Colin's ashes. It suddenly seems right.

The weather was perfect; brilliant azure-blue sky. Driving along the loke I had a deep conviction he was with me and also that he would not want me to wallow in gloom.

I was soon enveloped in a breathtaking Norfolk countryside; fields between Aylsham and Blakeney were tranquil and golden with hay rolls- a subject that was a favourite with buyers of his paintings. The whole way, sunshine shimmered and dipped through rich green foliage.

Eighty pence to park on the beach at Blakeney! I can imagine what Colin would have said.

I walked to a quiet peaceful part of the beach. The only sounds were seagulls crying and the soft singing of yacht rigging. In the distance, town and church peeped down to the sea.

The water was warm. I paddled through soft sand where the tide flowed out to wider seas. To everywhere. To all over the world wherever our sons might be. I scattered his ashes on the water. I told him how much we all loved him. I thanked him for our years together.

And so I celebrated his life with the sunshine and the sea.

When I looked down, shoals of tiny fishes swam around my feet. As a keen fisherman he would have liked that - and being part of the moving world.

On the way home I had a lovely lunch outside a pub at Blickling.

That night I prayed I'd chosen the right place for him. The next day I had a strange urge to return to Blakeney. The evening was serene. This time the tide was in. The scene was a replica of his last painting: a man on a yacht with red sails, disappearing on to a yellow horizon.

It felt to me as if he was in one of his own pictures.

I sat on a bench overlooking the estuary and happened to glance down. Beneath the bench was the name of the man who had made it. His address was "Freshwater" - a tiny place on the Isle of Wight.

Colin was born there.

19th July: Rest in peace, my love.

FIFTEEN

'It's time you were getting over things by now.'

My dad's deep know-all tone reasoned with me over the phone. In childhood the sound of his voice had put the fear of God into me and now, even though he was trying to be gentle, I didn't want to know. I hated that platitude anyway. "Getting over things" is something the bereaved will do in their own time and not when someone else thinks they should.

Relationships in families can be difficult enough without chucking in the spanner of bereavement.

I'd been to visit my parents in Derby and had behaved like a stiff stranger... one of those awful "firsts" without Colin to act as a buffer between dad and me. That first visit felt like a cross between the Prodigal Son and Barrie's Mary-Rose, but in the latter case, I'd changed and everyone else had stayed the same. My dad had greeted me warmly on the station with the words: 'It's nice to have you back in the family again.'

Taut and tired, I'd replied acidly, 'I never left it. I brought someone else into it. Remember?'

Colin and my father were chalk and cheese from the day Colin entered the house with a beard, open-toed sandals and no tie.

Dad liked to control his women. Colin didn't want to control anyone.

But, strangely, as the years went by and he taught dad to fish, a warmth developed between them and Colin handled him far better than I did. My relationship with dad had always been fiery. Unlike mum, a gentle little person whom everyone loved - and the only woman for my father.

I see now how difficult it must have been for everyone on that first visit. I loathed myself for being so distant, especially when dad saw me off at the station with a little box of goodies he'd lovingly arranged: chocolate - bars, grapes, orange, sweets. When I opened it in the train, tears fell relentlessly.

I could not begin to understand myself. As a parent I've made a mountain of mistakes I regret. And certainly as a daughter. I only know the relationship between me and those I really love is far too complex to unravel and I don't want to leave it until it's too late before I say, 'Look, I know we've had our differences, but... I love you.'

I love you.

We must tell one another. It really is all that matters. I remember Irene Handl once saying on radio, 'Cuddle while you can.' And when I see couples quarrelling, I long to repeat it to them.

So I returned to the cottage in a right old state! But only my diary knew.

Sunday: Ye gods. Whatever am I like? Went to church. Had forgotten how boring sermons can be. Don't know why I went unless for the company - one place a woman can go on her own without looking like a woman on her own. Sat mulling over the idea of selling the cottage. Could rent it, I suppose, but Pat told me of tenants who let their kids roller-skate on someone else's parquet floors. Heard a story about a man who left everything until tomorrow and then died before he could do anything. That's me. Prevaricating Prudence.

The tragedy queen bit was to last a long time, although I wasn't acting. I was like many widowed, grief-stricken, confused and extremely lonely. Writing it now is like watching a video of someone else's suffering. Every video is different. There are no rules. But how I would ban all those well meaning 'Pull yourself together' clichés. Actually, I'd ban all advice.

July 30th 1990: Received a lovely letter from May at Writers' Circle. She sent a set of prints Colin had drawn of the Old Norwich City Gates to friends who framed them and wrote to say how beautiful they looked. 'I thought you would like to know that, and how much pleasure they are going to continue to give people.' I did like to know that, May. How nice people are who bother to send cheering letters. Iris and I are always phoning one another. We bolster each other up. I often think of us larking about in the pantomime, neither knowing her husband was to die from a heart attack a few months later. I would go bats without the phone.

A widower rang to ask: 'How would you like to make up a foursome and come out with my girlfriend and me for a pub-meal?'

I hadn't been out with any man other than Colin in thirty-five years. I dug up excuses with mounting hysteria.

'Hold on - hold on!' he interrupted. 'Listen! You have to get out of that cottage. Now, be sensible; come and have a meal with us.'

After wallowing in a misery of indecision, I rang back to accept, as if to a funeral.

4th August 1990: I'm going out. I daren't think about Colin or I won't go.

But of course I did think about him. I saw him, tall, broad-shouldered and handsome in his suit, going out to start the car while I locked up and did "Off-offs" to switches. I saw him smile and say, 'You look nice.'

In hindsight I was hypersensitive. Daft, actually. Colin would have been pleased for me to be released from sobbing and brooding. As it was, I drove down the loke like a zombie.

The evening was delightful. I was introduced to a small dimpled widower who was merry and interesting. Once in the local pub, conversation and laughter reminded me there was a world outside I'd forgotten about.

The next day, I went back to church. I was absolutely fine until the vicar intoned, 'And now a prayer for the sad and bereaved.' I fled.

Did hell last forever?

6th August 1990: So flipping quiet out here. Tried that silly "Pull yourself together" lark. Back on sleeping tablets. Don't want to wake up again.

(I wondered about editing out such morbid diary entries, dismayed at how I gave in to misery and depression. But omitting them wouldn't have been honest. This is my true account showing how bereavement and isolation unbalanced me and how writing about such feelings helped me to eventually sort myself out. From talking to many widowed friends, I know others who have had similar or worse feelings in bereavement. We certainly aren't unique.)

7th August: This has got to stop. Is this what Colin would have wanted? He would not! I have three great sons. They are the part of him that is still alive. And I'm going the right way to orphan them. I have to go on. I won't quit. So it's… up your bum! Go for it! Even if I can only manage a day at a time; to live this one morning, this one hour. Martin's got it right. He said:

'Think of your pain as a headache that you're going to have for some time. Accept that. And accept that it will slowly get better.'

The next morning I made some bread and beat hell out of the dough.

12th August: Martin arrived; we took dog on beach at Blakeney. He gave me marvellous photos of Colin taken at my birthday last November. Such happy photos. I'm so lucky to have such memories. Am suddenly on a high. Won't slide back into the pit again. I have lived today.

13th August: Cruse. Joined some members afterwards for a pub-lunch.

God knows how I didn't murder anyone on the road during that awful year and I thank God for it. My concentration often lapsed. When Seán and his Greek girlfriend came to this country, I drove them to Derby, the first time I'd ever driven so far. When a pedestrian seemed as if she were about to cross at a crossing, even though traffic lights were green, in my favour, I stopped. Everything behind me scrunched to a halt. A lorry swerved into the middle of the road. Brakes for miles screeched.

I could hear Colin's expletive. And his son's, even louder. By the time we reached Derby I'd vowed never to drive again.

I decided to promote Colin's drawings, packed his cards and prints into a briefcase, dressed up in a business suit and carried them around Norwich. The National-Trust shop took some and paid me immediately. The Cathedral displayed them in their shop.

I felt a great sense of pride and joy to see his work on show again. I missed our exhibition days. And I felt I'd started a new phase of my life.

Greatly relieved I'd got the salesman bit over, I strolled around Norwich Cathedral. Soothing music was being played on the organ. To my intense frustration, tears coursed again down my cheeks. Was there to be no end to waterworks?

A nun escorted me into her small cell in the Cathedral. I bombarded her with questions I never knew were burning inside me:

'Why did he have to die with so much left to give? Why am I left to go on living? What sort of God did this? And if the spirit continues to live after death, how can he bear to see me like this? And why haven't I got the same courage others show...? '

I expected answers like a child demands attention.

All I really wanted was to have Colin back again.

Two years later I saw the same nun in the Cathedral coffee shop. To my dry-eyed (believe it!) astonishment she said, 'June Sutton?'

Such a sweet sound our own names have.

My daughter-in-law, Julie, who is very practical, showed me what went on inside my fuse-box when she and Paul visited: 'Keep torches handy, mum, in case of power-cuts.'

Paul showed me how to set a mousetrap. Mice were forever

lumbering like elephants in the loft at nights. I had an awful job setting those traps and was amazed someone hadn't invented a contraption that left your fingers and thumbs intact.

I laughed at memories of Colin, stalking the bedroom in the early hours, wearing only socks and carrying a golf club, after a mouse ran behind the wardrobe.

6th September: Tamba is daft. At dog training each dog had to perform individually off the lead. The minute I unclipped her she ran away ignoring all commands and skidded the entire length of the slippery floor. The teacher said severely to everyone, 'Please don't laugh. Some dogs like to play the clown and this is one of them.' But that laughter did me a power of good!

SIXTEEN

Sex can be a joyful part of a relationship. So why are we reluctant to talk about it after death separates us? I met many widowed men and women and we talked about everything else but no one mentioned sex - and I didn't. And yet it had been a very important part of my marriage.

For the first months after Colin died, my insides atrophied. Then, besides in every other way, I began to miss him sexually. Sex had been fun, in the bedroom - and just about everywhere else in or out of the cottage. The rambling garden was entirely private except for occasional helicopters buzzing above. We spent hot summer days naked like Adam and Eve out there... I remember laughing and warning Colin not to wield secateurs with such abandon as he pruned apple trees.

Oh, yes, I missed sex with him. And the hugs, kisses and handholding (we'd sit idiotically clutching one another in front of television). And I missed all the soppy things we said to one another.

One summer night, six months after Colin died, I tried to satisfy myself, imagining desperately that he was in bed with me. Immediately afterwards, great wracking sobs convulsed me.

Masturbation itself caused me no guilt. My gentle husband had been a wise and foreseeing man. Towards the end of his life, which up to then had been fulfilling sexually, blood-pressure tablets slowed down his system.

'We'll look in there,' he said when we passed a sex shop in London.

Through yellow bead curtains were all manner of fancy toys.

'Crikey!' I whispered. 'Just look at those!'

He laughed. 'Practical though.'

We had always discussed things together, including pleasing one another.

Years later, when I was having lunch with other widows, one of them said with a laugh, 'I couldn't have cared less about the sex side. I used to lie back and think of England.'

So, once again, we are all different - and she wasn't going to miss it, I suppose.

One of the most sensible articles I read on the subject was by the editors of Cruse Chronicle, a newsletter of the organisation for bereaved people. The following are some excerpts from it:

Sexual Feelings after the death of a Partner.

 Of the multitude of losses that we feel after the death of our partner, our husband, wife or lover, perhaps the one that friends and family are often most reluctant to recognise is the loss of physical love - of being held, touched and wanted because we are a loved and sexually desirable man or woman.

 ... It would be strange if our sexual feelings were to remain unaffected when our partner dies. Why should we expect this one part of ourselves to be immune to the ever-changing pressures of grief which affect so many other aspects of our life? The initial shock of death may numb all senses for a while , so that our sexual feelings may disappear in the hollowness of disbelief and despair. Or, as bereavement

loosens our sense of being in control of ourselves and the world around us, we might find ourselves spinning out of control in our sexual feelings and we could find that we are filled with desires we have not experienced for many years. This could surprise and confuse us, possibly leaving us pleased in some ways, in others guilty or ashamed.

It may not be easy to share such feelings with those around us because they are the sort of feelings which some people do not expect from those who are grieving. So we could find ourselves facing both the taboo which surrounds death, and the taboo of accepting and talking about our own and other people's sexuality.

In the months following our bereavement we may have to confront the problem of what to do with our sexual feelings. This is not a problem restricted to the young: sexual desires are not likely to disappear with increasing age, although they do tend to decrease in many people . Whether or not we have a partner, we continue to be a man or woman; it is still natural to feel physically attracted to others, to want to be loved and held and to feel sexual desires. Both men and women may find satisfaction in masturbation; this will not fill the aching void left after the death of a partner but it can bring a welcome relief from tension...

It is easy to drift into a sexual relationship when we are confused and vulnerable -- the white knight gallops over the horizon to mend our leaking roof; the kindly neighbour cooks a casserole and stays talking late into the night. If we have been bereaved fairly recently we may, perhaps unconsciously, be searching desperately for our partner who has died, and can all too easily slip into a search for a replacement lover or even someone to share a marriage or long-term relationship. How hard it can be to separate the longing to be held safe like a small, hurt child from the need for a long-term, loving sexual relationship with another person.

*One of the problems with new relationships formed in
these shifting sands of early grief is that they rarely survive,
and endings can be painful. This may or may not matter;
sometimes a one night stand or a short, good-natured relationship where both people have realistic expectations of each
other can bring great pleasure, comfort, and sense of hope
when everything seems hopeless. But if we have been hoping
for an 'instant' new relationship which would mean as much
to us as the one which ended through the death of our
partner, we are almost bound to be disappointed...*

*...Ultimately our sexuality lies deep within us.
Although grief may blanket our desires for a while, or
diminish our ability to control them; although life may not
present us with an opportunity to make love; although each
year we grow a little older, the fact that we are a man or a
woman will always remain a vital part of what we are... At
some point we may have to give ourselves permission to move
forward, to let go of the past and live for the present and the
future. This may be a future shared with a new partner and
an additional set of relations. On the other hand we may
find, quite unexpectedly, that we reach a stage where we are
truly able to live alone; that there is a new pleasure in
conquering new tasks and solving new challenges, in discovering sides to our character that we never knew existed.
Living alone may offer us a sense of independence and oppor-
tunities for fulfilment which suit us well.*

Reading the article helped me realise my feelings were normal. I iden-
tified with other aspects, too; I was vulnerable and at a later date, made
some daft mistakes.

To begin with, only keeping busy did me any good. I wanted to start
writing novels again but that meant solitude and I hated my own
company. Besides the shock-block in my brain hadn't thawed out. I
remember, years before, exclaiming gauchly to Mary Ingate, past

President of Norwich Writers' Circle and Crime Novelist of the year: 'Oh, you mustn't give up writing, Mary, that would be an awful waste,' after her husband died.

Until it happens to us we cannot know.

The secretary of a local group lost her husband and a month later was asked by a committee member if she could resume her duties. The member said to me, 'After all, it's four weeks since her husband died... and the company might do her good.'

Until it happens to us we cannot know.

I had reached the stage of indulging in aimless hyperactivity but there was no way I wanted to return to groups who'd known both Colin and me. I don't know why. Instead, I volunteered to work in a newly formed charity shop in a small town. Other assistants were on first-name terms. We weren't a group of strangers coming together. I was the stranger. And I felt it. I would, wouldn't I? I was Mrs Hypersensitivity.

Searching for - I don't know what - I then joined an Adult Education course on greenhouses. I was not in the least bit interested in greenhouses. Except I'd been left one. At one point I asked a question of the teacher.

'I've already told you that,' he said in a severe over-the-spectacles manner.

At break-time I scuttled out for coffee and did not return that session.

Widowed friends understood about such temperamental weaknesses. One was a friend who had overdosed and, after treatment, took up voluntary work and became brighter, prettier and more positive.

'I'm having a dinner-party. Why don't you come?' she asked me. 'It will do you good.'

When she said that, I knew she knew what she was talking about. But for all sorts of potty reasons I made excuses. Visiting socially without Colin held little pleasure. I'd be the spectre at the wedding. (I'm amazed anyone asked me anywhere!)

'If you change your mind, June, come along.'

On the evening of the party I sat indoors chewing my fingers. There was a great crack of thunder and rain lashed against the cottage. I couldn't make up my mind whether it was more miserable to stay indoors or launch myself into the weather. I decided the former was. I showered and dressed up in the swirly Miss Selfridge dress Colin had bought me for my birthday.

'I am going out,' I shouted, doing a solitary twirl.

I'm not kidding - at that exact moment, the largest window in the sitting room shattered. Shards of glass splattered across the carpet inside and the lawn outside. I stared open-mouthed at the huge jagged hole that was left; at curtains whipped wildly by the gale, at rain belting in from all angles.

Was it a message? I wished there'd been a telephone link with heaven.

Shock, anger and raging winds fired me. I didn't bloody well ask to be left alone in the cottage. And nothing, especially a rotten lousy storm was going to dictate the way I ran my life.

I bumped a great lump of block-board we had used as a table-tennis top down the stairs, one awkward step at a time. It was too heavy to lift up to the sitting room windowsill so I raised it using a combination of stools and chairs, a little at a time. Once it was lodged against the remaining glass, I pinned stapled drawing paper, dustbin liners and cardboard in an odd pattern around gaps. And closed the curtains. Rain still gusted in but much less of it. Anyway, sod perfection. I tucked wide swirls of navy jersey dress into my knickers and began collecting heaps of glass slivers bedded in the carpet. I got angry again. This was my best frock. I'd spent ages hyping myself up to go to this dinner-party... the mess could wait until morning.

I flung open the cottage-door.

'Come on, Tam. We're going out.'

The dog eyed sheeting rain and slunk back into bed.

'Out!'

She sashayed from the kitchen and into the car like a reluctant ballet-dancer.

Every country lane was flooded. I drove, glassy-eyed through deep pools of water that sloshed against the car. I didn't care if I broke down. I didn't care about anything, like stalling the car and being jumped at by some poor soul lurking sodden behind a hedge (as if). Nothing mattered.

As for the dinner-party - it was great. The meal was lovely and afterwards we sang round a piano - and danced. Everyone suggested the best places to go to get my window repaired, so I came away well satisfied and very pleased I'd got myself sorted and driven out into the gale.

It was a salutary lesson for me when I met M only last month. M is in her sixties and I think about her when I'm being a wimp. She told me that a few years ago, after her husband died, she bought a round-the-world-ticket and backpacked herself to New Zealand. Her daughter arranged for her to stay somewhere on her first night but after that she was on her own, arranging to stay in hotels and hostels. On one flight she sat next to a man who was friendly but inebriated and at one point said, 'Are you my wife?' She saw beautiful sights and walked miles alone, often into solitary places.

I admired her courage and self-motivation. But I could not make up my mind whether she had been incredibly brave or foolhardy to visit some doubtful areas alone.

'But you see, I didn't care,' she said.

This year she has been on two holidays on her own and is obviously happy with her own company.

'But I had to make myself do it at the beginning, June. And sometimes I was ever so tired afterwards.'

I'm proud to know her.

1st October 1990: Mice rampaging through attics. Shopped for traps and paint. I reckon big DIY stores are useless for women on their own. I get more help and advice from smaller stores. Met L. at Cruse. She started to train as a counsellor after her husband died but found it too gruelling. They usually advise you to wait two years after bereavement before thinking about that.

'There are too many walking-wounded around us, too tired and unhappy to make an effort to do anything,' she said. ' You know - Colin is still with you. He is there between the split seconds in a way we can't understand.' I believe her. She said, 'When our husbands were alive, they were the focus of our lives. We rarely put ourselves first. It's important we learn to please ourselves now. Love ourselves.'

A young widower at Cruse told me his brother told him to pull himself together. He said he'd got pains in his legs and the doctor told him it was brought on by grief. That damn "Pull yourself together"! The effect of bereavement on another man there has been awful. He can't speak and only communicates by writing notes. I admire the saintly patient people who stay with him.

When I got home I wrote the word FIGHT on my cheese-board and hung it on the wall. Then I ate three Kit-Kats and washed the greenhouse. As I dislodged moss the door came off its runners. Left the blooming thing to be fixed by the first hefty bloke who comes up here. Big laugh! Colin's male colleagues are only noticeable by their absence. Fixed a pipe so water from greenhouse runs into a butt.

Martin rang. It appears thespians can begin to take on the roles they act, so if I act cheerfully, I may start to feel cheerful. Laughter has a beneficial effect on the body's immune system, producing endorphins. Looked it up in dictionary: endorphin - opiate-like substance with pain-killing properties.

All I need now is something to laugh at.

2nd October: Boiler went out. I hate the bloody thing. Took hours to relight.

7th October: Loathe Sundays. Family day. Watched David Attenborough trilogy about animal births. Brief moment in time. That's what we are. Tiny blink of an eyelid. Each and every one of us. Colin once said I'd never be able to stay here on my own, but I've been here for eight months. How much longer? He promised never to leave me here alone at night.

So are you here, Colin, in the split seconds?

8th October: Counsellor at Cruse asked me if I'd consider being on the committee as a representative of the group. Don't feel capable of being anybody's rotten representative. Anyway, scared stiff to drive on my own at night. Never driven to that part of Norwich. Found leaflet Colin had left in boiler room on the workings of the boiler. Good. Had a look in toilet cistern. Screws holding it on wall look mightily rusty to me. What would I do if it fell off? Turn off water? Must find stop-tap. No hefty man imminent so sprayed WD40 on greenhouse door. Got it back on runners. Jumped for pure joy!

After that, whenever I visited folk I'd go to the lavatory and take the lid off the cistern to see what their screws were like.

Now, whenever I left the cottage for a few days it always felt good to be back. I could wander about in the night without disturbing anyone. But then, after a few days, deep dreadful depression would set in. Made me wonder if it was worth breaking the established routine. But neither did I want to become a hermit. Pam said she got through the weeks by looking forward to her next holiday. If she hadn't arranged one she didn't want to be bothered getting up in a morning.

27th October 1990: Colin's birthday. The first without you, my love. The pain of loving you, missing you and needing you is unbearable. Time can never heal this wound.

It was another of those "firsts" to be got over. I was so thankful the children came home. We celebrated, as Colin would have liked. We celebrated his life.

29th October: Had a panic attack in night. Thought they were over! Kept wondering if I could have done more to help you, Colin. Tried to pray. Nothing there. Nothing but silence. Thought Jesus was supposed to answer prayer? If one of my kids asked me for help, I'd do my very best to comfort him. Or am I missing something here?

It would have been so easy to pine away. I had to keep busy. That was best. After the greenhouse course I went to a D.I.Y. course. The first afternoon I learned how to wire a doorbell.

11th November: I am here in Church, writing and managing to sit through a Remembrance-Day service without crying. But I don't know what I'm doing here. Has the Church survived for so many centuries simply because people need to believe in something? Is it all in the mind? Or is Christ truly alive? He hasn't helped me. I don't know anything. And I don't know if I can survive for much longer without Colin. He was me.

The following week I heard a presenter on Radio Norfolk say helpers were needed for The Gateway Club, a group for people with learning disabilities, or it would have to close.

I entered the Centre apprehensively. I'd had no experience with such adults.

'Hello-o.'

A small dark man shuffled across and gave me a big hug.

I sat in on activities. The organiser was giving a talk on First Aid. She was explaining how to do mouth-to-mouth resuscitation. The place oozed love and warmth. I was to become used to Harold bombarding me with, 'Hello. How are you? What's your name?' every few minutes. Or Rosie putting her arms around me. I was accepted as I was, lonely, bewildered and probably sick.

The next day I travelled to the Barbican Centre to see Paul receive his Diploma in Architecture. Such emotions. I was so incredibly proud. As I know Colin would have been. He'd have told everyone. Paul had accomplished what Colin himself had wanted to achieve. I was there for both of us. But Colin was there, too.

19th November: There's a woman at Cruse whose husband died of cancer, who is always serene and smiling. She said, 'My husband had a terrific sense of humour. Every day I look at his photo and say, "Gertcha!"' I've been forgetting all the times Colin made me cry with laughter, haven't I? What with all this self-pity and stuff.

DIY classes improved. I learned about Rawlplugs and drilled into every available surface including bricks. It was good fun. One man there said he never went away for any length of time without turning off his water. Found my mains water-tap. Covered in cobwebs. But it turned.

In November I walked miles through crackling frosty fields with Tamba. I constantly told myself how lucky I was to have known such love in my life and should let that thought underpin my future.

My niece rang, 'Get your butt down to Derby this Christmas, Aunty.'
Christmas? I didn't even want to think about Christmas.

I. rang to tell me she'd had a dreadful week crying.

'I sat on the stairs thinking, who can I call? I didn't want to upset my family. So I thought, I'll call June.'

We need a detached voice to listen to us. The telephone was my godsend when I was desperate. And listening to other people may have made me cry for them, but it focussed my thoughts on someone else besides me.

The second time I went to Gateway, I decided to contribute something to the afternoon's activities and took a Keep-Fit session. I congratulated myself when they all enjoyed moving to music so much.

'Do you want to do it again?' I asked eagerly.

'No - o - o!' they chorused (or was it a groan?). So I got stuck into cooking their beans on toast. Mind, weeks later, Harold grinned widely, stretched out his arms and enthused, 'I did this with you.'

Those damned panic attacks! One night I was convinced - again - I was having a heart attack but I didn't dare bring the doctor bumping across fields for nothing. I rang the Samaritans again:

'Will you please take my name and address? I'm frightened I'm going to collapse and no one will find me for days.'

Someone called Desmond talked calmly to me until my heart stopped racing. Thank you Desmond. I was able to sleep again.

Each time viewers came to look over the cottage I felt unhappy and most muddled. Martin explained to me about Tao... to go with the flow he said. It worked - for a few hours. But a few hours at a time was okay.

One dragon I had to slay was my nervousness about driving at night otherwise my life was going to be drastically curtailed. First I took the car along to my garage to have it serviced and make sure it would not be likely to break down while I was out. I'd always relied on Colin to rescue me when that happened.

It was a brilliant garage and the owner was kindness itself. Thank God for him, I thought. I was finding myself thanking a God I didn't believe in for a variety of, what had become for me, life-saving activities.

So off I went driving into the city one dark wet night. On the return journey I passed another car in a narrow lonely lane when there was an enormous bang. Like an explosion. Further along I stopped and climbed out. My wing-mirror had shattered, obviously having collided with the other car's wing-mirror.

As a woman alone I was uncertain about what to do. I suppose I should have climbed back in the car, locked doors and windows and driven to meet my opponent. As it was, I got away.

The next day I took the car into my garage to have the mirror replaced.

'That was my mother you hit,' said the owner.

SEVENTEEN

As I read diaries now I first wrote in 1990 after Colin died, the ups and downs of grief are all too apparent. One either copes or goes under. I wavered between the two in a limbo many will recognise.

5th December 1990: Snowstorms forecast - have food in for a siege. Marvellous atmosphere at Gateway with carol singing and percussion instruments. People with learning disabilities often have such warmth and affection. Christmas without Colin will be horrendous but Gateway's joyous rumbustious bell-ringing festivities followed by country dancing were a million miles removed from death.

10th December: Paul's birthday… memories of a breech birth in Woking hospital. It all happened to another person, another life. My first baby - such a love. I did my Christmas card list, searching through Colin's notebook. I'd like to sleep until this shopkeeper's bonanza is over. "Pick yourself up, dust yourself down and start all over again," kept being played on radio. Hate it. I am so very tired, but haven't done anything. There must be more than this emptiness. Where are ghosts?

11th December: Sat up most of the night doing crosswords. Will I ever sleep again? There is really only one sleep I need. Feel very odd. Don't want to see anyone. Stayed in my bedroom all day.

13th December: Silent night. Silent cottage. Stayed in bedroom. No sun, no moon, no you, no me… if I'm really here. Perhaps I'm not. Perhaps this is all happening to someone else.

15th December: Such depression.

16th December: Last night I dreamed I was flying through clouds with Colin, begging him to let me stay with him, hanging on to his rigid body. We saw the world in seconds, great ochre coloured cliffs and wide green valleys. I dreamed I woke up still holding on to him. He wasn't dead after all. It had all been a terrible mistake. That part was lovely. I clung to him, told him he was never out of my thoughts. But as the dream progressed he grew old and weak before my eyes and I woke up. How selfish of me to hang on to him. Clingy clingy clingy. How on earth do I purge my lousy subconscious longings to drag him back? I still remember vividly the night before the funeral when I dreamed he asked me to go with him and held out his hands to me. No words can ever express my emotions when I think about the inexplicable moment I hesitated. And he vanished.

17th December: Our Wedding anniversary. A counsellor offered to counsel me again. Sod that. I haven't progressed at all from last time. I'm a total mess.

18th December: Bad bad bad. Why didn't I think to change his wet pants before they took him away?

As I read this now I feel relieved I had enough sense in the midst of madness to get me to a doctor. I was sitting in the waiting room after-wards whilst tablets were dispensed and saw the wife of a director. She spoke to me in hushed tones about another director at the firm:

'Have you heard? They found him sitting in his chair the next morning. He'd had a heart attack.' She added in a whisper: 'Just like Colin.'

So passed a first Christmas without him. The year before we'd spent it on our own. On Christmas Eve we went for a meal at a hotel in Norwich and were the first couple in the restaurant with only one other couple arriving later. We pulled crackers, wore paper-hats and threw streamers... the only kids in the playground. I thought it was awful.

But that's before I knew what really mattered in life.

I spent 1990 Christmas Day in Derby with Pat and Ken who cosseted me with love, kindness and daffodils and accommodated my children.

'Married couples will partner one another in this game,' announced a guest, unthinking.

'You come with us, mum,' Paul and Martin chimed in unison.

The homeward journey was less than jolly with no water in the train washbasins but toilet paper floating in sodden streamers across the floor.

31st, December 1990: The worst year of my life is over. Found a crumpled hanky in Colin's dressing gown pocket and buried my face in it. Now I wait for sleeping tablets to obliterate my senses.

EIGHTEEN

1990 was finished. Not only the saddest year of my life but also the most self-pitying, the most angry. But there must have been a seed of hope hidden in my unconscious, dictating I could make it if I stuck it out. So like many others in my position I carried on again, as Sydney Smith, a Yorkshire Rector suggested, by taking short views of human life - "not further than dinner or tea. Be as busy as you can."

The next crisis was always lurking around the bend (crises only stop happening when we are dead). One trick... if you had the energy... was to think ahead and have names and addresses of skilled people handy who could help with practical matters. As for emotional outbursts - I believe they're our safety valves until we begin to get better.

We British are not very good at "letting go." We have to be given permission. Only today I read a glowing report in one newspaper, heaping praise on a widow because of her composure at her husband's funeral. Instinctively I wished I could have been more composed at Colin's. It's all that military influence behind us; the stiff-upper lip brigade who frown at wailing and gnashing of teeth.

Jack, a widower declares stalwartly, 'Of course we don't crack up. Not in this country. How do you think we won all those battles? Soldiers' wives didn't let their feelings show when their husbands were killed. They were proud their men had defended the country.'

Maybe. But it was better for me to cry loudly or beat hell out of bread-dough or scream as I drove my car along the mud track to the cottage, rather than let grief fester silently inside me.

Four years after her husband died, Jeanette said she wished there were somewhere she could go to scream really loudly. 'I thought about going on the roller-coaster at Yarmouth Funfair,' she said. This was a woman who helped many others who had been bereaved. Because she understood. And cared.

Before Jeanette and many like her became my friends, I was a lost soul and felt particularly so one filthy wet blustery night when Colin's car broke down on me for the first time. When he'd been alive, and I drove off in my old banger, he'd say, 'Remember to phone me before you come home and if you aren't back in a reasonable time, I'll drive out to look for you.' (Such cosseting! And why the heck hadn't I flung flowers at his feet every time he said it?)

Now I sat panic-stricken at green traffic lights near Norwich Airport while a great queue of traffic built up behind me in the storm. And I could hear Colin's voice telling me - like ET - to phone home. Only there was no one at home. There never would be.

Two men pushed the car on to the forecourt of a little shoe-shop. Customers stared as I hurried inside to phone for roadside assistance. They thought it was rain dripping down my face (those shop assistants in there were the kindest I've ever known).

The AA man fixed the car: 'I'll follow you home to make sure she doesn't cut out again,' he said.

I settled down to drive along the busy main road. But I still couldn't block the voice in my head. I became a sobbing disaster. I was driving blind and safety dictated I drew in to the kerb. The AA man ran from his car and peered in through the pouring rain.

'Has she gone again?'

I told him I couldn't see traffic ahead. He waited while I blew my nose and got myself together.

Widowed friends have told me they'd be going along fine; beginning to cope with exhaustion and grief, then, without warning something would remind them of him/her and it was down into the abyss again feeling lost and forsaken.

It's like an illness. Each one of us has to find his/her own way of clawing back to mental and physical health. And there is help to be found if we look. So blow continually parading that brave face.

I tried to remember difficult episodes in our marriage thinking it might help ease the loss. Colin was no saint and sometimes I drove him potty. I remember him chucking a big breakfast cup at the kitchen door once after we argued. It was a rare fling for a normally moderate self-controlled man.

Our first two years together were fiery as we adjusted to one another's ways. We were such different characters from different backgrounds. It took time to gel, for love to consolidate and round corners into curves of reason.

I once tried to leave him when Paul was a baby. Even then we lived in a remote spot in the middle of a wood. It was suggested, after the birth in Woking hospital in December, that we stay with my mother-in-law who lived nearby, until I got on my feet. She was a lively intelligent woman and I was much in awe of her. But go there with my new baby...?

After a while, I believe I had what is now called "Post Natal Depression" but in those days you just got on with things. I remember missing my own mother and once, after an argument (can't remember what about) I caught a taxi to the local railway station, intending to go to my parents' home in Derby.

A short while later I stood desolately on Waterloo Station with the baby wrapped in a white lace shawl and suddenly wondered what the hell I was doing? There was no way I could leave Colin. I loved him too much. I hated him as well. But that passed.

Safely back and trauma over, I realised the three of us being together was bliss.

After he died it was comforting to talk on the phone with his sister, Audrey, about daft family times. It was another link with him. Sometimes I'd bawl, 'I can't go on without him.'

'Come on. Colin didn't marry a wimp,' she'd remonstrate. She too would need all her strength. Within a few years she lost her mother, father, brother and husband.

We must accept that life is cruelly unfair.

14th January 1991: Driving to Cruse and the stupid car conked out again. Didn't cry this time, I was too angry. Out came the very nice man again. Have booked the damned car into my garage. Hope owner's mother isn't there! Gulf War seems inevitable now. All peace missions have failed. I think sanctions should be given more time to work because so many young people are going to be killed. God knows what's going to happen now.

In bed I listened to the radio when the liberation of Kuwait began. Bombing in Baghdad. Security had been stepped up at British Airports. It gave me something other than myself to think about in the middle of the night.

Panic set in again the next morning when I received a letter from the Gas Board. They intended to run a gas-line across the fields to RAF Coltishall. It would cross the loke and my precious water pipe. Resolutions about taking everything calmly were forgotten. Where was Colin now with his efficiency and expertise? I wanted him. I needed him! And why the hell did my sons have to live so far away? I studied the letter closely. Did I own the track or have right of way? My letter. My water-pipe. My problem.

17th January: My book: "The Silent Witness" has been sold Greek Rights for £300. I receive half. I shall be rich! Haven't time to write, not by the time I've taken the dog out, done the boiler etc. (how I hate solid fuel). How on earth did Colin manage to go out to work and paint? Iraq has fired a missile at Israel. Bad news.

18th January: Alarm went off last night and it wasn't even set. Read Colin's notes in his file about how deep the water pipe was. Also read: Always remember to include, "Subject to Contract" when buying a property. Shall I sell and let somebody else sort out the blasted water pipe? Bought some calming herbal pills.

19th January: Long to meet people on the same wavelength as me, just as Colin was.

I made an effort and invited three friends for lunch. Now, I had to think about setting the table... no slouching in an armchair picking from a plastic pack. I hadn't realised how grubby the cottage was and spent forever cleaning. The resulting tidiness and unusual smell of polish made me feel much better even though I'm not very housewifely.

Preparing the meal had been as exhausting as preparing a banquet but I looked back on it with a feeling of achievement. I hadn't wasted the day. And we'd talked about Colin and laughed at memories. That was nice.

I bounced to Cruse on Monday feeling brighter. A widower asked me if I would go out with him? It threw me. I still hated the thought. I refused because I hadn't the sensitivity to see that he, too, was lonely and unhappy. I turned down the opportunity to help and be helped.

My widowed friend Peggy and I went along to Norwich Sports Village and hired a snooker-table and cues. Neither of us knew the rules but some teenage boys showed us where to position the balls. We didn't pot any but had a delicious lunch afterwards.

Getting out was what it was all about.

6th February 1991: Chill factor 10 with snow forecast. Please God don't let me be cut off. Why must farmers take hedges out? Scrambled up into loft and couldn't get down for ages. Ice in header-tank. Left trap door open like Colin did so warmth from cottage could penetrate. Not as though the flipping boiler is burning well - hardly any heat in radiators. Carted five hods of coke and coal into the back-porch in case snow falls. Rang Iris for a chat. Her neighbours asked her round for the evening saying it wasn't a night for her to be on her own. Radio reports

Siberian winds. Twenty thousand call-outs to the AA. Kent and Surrey hit very badly. Never in my worst dreams did I envisage a situation where I'd be left alone here.

It was YOU who wanted to come here, Colin!

8th February: I'm now cut off from the world. Can't get down loke. Neither can all the thousands of friends who will no doubt want to come and see me. Woke at 2.00 am and made tea. Terrible night.. Christine in village rang to ask if I wanted any shopping. Nice surprise, but she is a nice woman. South of country hit badly: 12 inches of snow in Essex. This is what I've been dreading the most. I walk around the cottage talking to Colin. I tell myself he believed in me and I must believe in me. I can cope!

9th February: Audrey said her friend in America sent me a message that she envied me because I didn't have to watch Colin suffer. Her husband suffered so long.

12th February: The sun is shining! Yippee! And I managed to drive down the loke! Tamba was skittering around with a frog's leg dangling from her mouth.
WE MADE IT!

13th February: Civilians killed in Baghdad. Americans bombed their shelter because it was being used for military purposes. This time next year will anyone remember about this war? I found my granddad's war-medal in a drawer. He must have been Paul's age when he died. What in heaven's name is it all about? Marrying, giving birth, bringing up kids, letting them go, hoping they'll keep in touch. Dying. But we're all dying.

Jottings in a diary may have helped me emotionally, but it couldn't help me make decisions. Not as though I've ever been any good at that. What seemed a good idea one minute soured the next. But at last I actually made up my mind to get cracking and leave the cottage for a month to try and sort out my thoughts.

My niece told me of a house I could rent next door to her in Derby.

148

It was only used at holiday times by a couple who'd bought it for their retirement.

A complete change of scenery, eh? Worth considering.

'The only snag is, Auntie June, it's sparsely furnished and has no carpets or phone.'

Well, that wouldn't matter for a month, would it? It was a chance to have a break and take the dog, too. There would be people, shops, newspapers put through the door, milk delivered… and it wasn't a big decision, like selling up.

'You'll be OK to drive, Mum. Honestly.' Martin gave me another of his tapes on positive thinking.

But the thought still frightened me. Unfortunately it was the only way I was going to transport dog, typewriter, clothes, sink…

My youngest son also had a fund of wise sayings and one helped me enormously on the dreaded drive… "The six P's: Perfect Planning Prevents Piss-Poor Performance".

I spent hours studying the route; drew numerous miniature diagrams to stick in order on the dashboard, each one to be ripped off as I passed that landmark.

I didn't want to leave Colin's precious paintings in the empty cottage. I phoned Lloyds Bank. They would store them in their vaults.

I wheeled Colin's large trolley through Norwich with the pictures locked in a case on it. A guy at Lloyds took the case to store it.

'How do you know I haven't got a bomb in there?' I said.

If he took my case on trust, what about other people's containers? I had money on a deposit account with them. He only smiled. I expect they had ways of scanning them.

Two days before driving to the Midlands, I disgorged the boot of the car looking for the spare tyre and jack, neither of which I'd ever laid eyes on. It was like a treasure hunt. To my surprise, I discovered a well under the carpet in the boot where both tyre and jack lay in snugly pristine condition.

I told my subconscious - which always got to work at night - I was OK and ready to travel. Of course I woke with a panic attack. My left arm hurt dreadfully and I felt sick. Definitely heart. I got up, brewed tea and tried to read. I told myself it was all in my imagination, but I knew I was a gonner. As ever, I was astonished when I woke the next morning.

The day before leaving I packed the car, cramming it to its limits with all my stuff, plus blankets and bed for the dog. I then wrote in my diary:

23rd February 1991: I don't want to do this rotten drive. I really do not. I'm missing Colin so badly. To hell with pi sayings about being able to handle anything that comes my way.

Fear was rampant. The next morning I was sick. If I hadn't already packed the car I wouldn't have gone. But I didn't have the energy to unpack. I lay down until rooms stopped spinning and eventually got away at nine a.m. First I said a prayer that I wouldn't do anything silly or hurt anyone. Then I said aloud, 'Wherever you are, wherever you be, Colin walk along'a me.'

As often happened, I wasn't quite sure to whom I was praying.

I made myself concentrate by talking aloud about road signs I passed and chewing soft-mints. I got through packets while scouring roads ahead. At Kings Lynn there was a nasty big roundabout with traffic lights. It was a stinker. I'd never been on one like it. And a police-car drove behind me.

'Where the hell do we go, Tamba?'

But she was fast asleep in the back.

Later, instead of switching to the A17 I circumnavigated another island twice and took the A47 to Wisbech instead (that police-car hadn't helped.)

Don't panic! I carried on until I reached the end of a no-stopping zone and then read the map and discovered I could take a cross-country route back to the A 17. I drove through pretty winding lanes and pastoral settings with fields and ponds. I was able to give the mints a rest.

On the A17 I stopped for my first break. With legs like deflating tyres I veered into Arthur's Cafe and had a bacon sandwich and coffee. I don't know if it was elation at getting back on the pre-ordained route, or knowing the journey was half done, but that sandwich tasted better than any I've ever had.

I'd been dreading driving through Nottingham but roads were really well signposted and with only a few heart-stopping moments we were soon on the A52 to Derby.

My lovely sister had been living the journey with me. She said she'd be waiting near a bridge on the Spondon Bypass so I could follow her through a maze of roads to their house.

I saw her standing in the pouring rain. I don't know how long she'd been there. I drew into a lay-by.

I climbed out of the car and we put our arms around one another. We were both crying.

The journey had taken over five hours. BUT I'D DONE IT! I'D DONE IT!

NINETEEN

This is really great, I thought.

I inspected the house I was renting. Tamba could run free in a fenced garden. Gas central heating meant no hods of coke to carry. I got excited when a newspaper rattled through the door and milk was delivered. I could wash the pots and watch children walking to school, neighbours working in gardens and tradesmen passing. Roads were lined with cars in spite of slim garages and smart young couples chatting over them, heads bobbing.

This was a civilisation I had forgotten.

Tamba skittered across the shiny uncarpeted floor, slid into sliding floor-to-ceiling windows and stunned herself.

5th March 1991: Have been here a week. Dad said he'd asked a man to give him details of a property not far from them that he thought I might be interested in buying...

I expected to find peace of mind once I'd left the cottage but the yo-yo syndrome returned. Mornings were fine. I loved being able to walk to shops, mingle with folk, see relatives - but at night, once I'd shut my door I discovered for the first time the horror of being alone without a phone.

Soon, I needed help again. I enquired about Derby Cruse but was told they only met once a fortnight. I'd ring Iris and Peggy in Norwich from telephone kiosks. Just to talk. I was in no-man's land. Even the Derby dialect sounded strange. And I've got one.

12th March: I can understand now how moving house, especially to a new area could be a shaker. And I don't know where I'd go if I did sell. I've no relatives and only a few friends in Norwich. Still too soon maybe?

I gradually established a routine in the echoing carpet-less rooms.

'Scram,' I'd warn Tamba as she padded across wide wet floors I'd super-mopped with Flash. I crammed the weeny downstairs cloaks with brushes and buckets, realising just how much storage space I'd got at the cottage compared to this brand new house.

'That's a nice little bungalow I told you about,' persisted my dad.

I decided my best bet was to explore the area to look at property for myself, even if it was only to discover what I didn't want because I sure as hell didn't know what I did want. Anything was better than moping about mopping. And it was something positive... Martin would have approved.

I bought a map of Derbyshire, filled a flask and toured with Tamba.

What stunned me was the flying freedom I felt once I was up in the Derbyshire hills. I was actually homesick for the country! And the Peak District is superb. From Bakewell to Buxton, Dovedale to Ashbourne, it would be difficult to beat.

I collected property details from estate agents.

'You don't want a three bedroomed house!' my dad declared.

But I had visions of family and grandchildren not yet born, queuing to visit. It's easy to delude ourselves the chicks will flutter back. Of course they must build their own lives and so should we. It's only recently I've faced that fact and chucked out spare beds and mattresses.

But I did know I wanted a spare bedroom and a study. (So I was getting there.)

I soon discovered you couldn't run away from self or grief.

20th March: Last night I had another panic-attack. To be alone is bad enough. To be alone without a phone is wacky! The only way I could have got help in an emergency was by unlocking windows and screaming into the night air. OK, so I'm wallowing again in self-pity. And I don't give six sodding wet handkerchiefs. Today I wasn't hanging around indoors clip-clopping across bare floors. Drove in the pouring rain to Swarkestone Bridge and walked beside the murky river with Tamba.

Swarkestone Bridge... where I used to spend sunny summer days, swimming and picnicking when I was a little girl. But now childhood was a blur. Marriage had changed me forever. I'd fallen for a man like no other I'd met - a free spirit who believed in each person's basic right to think and speak for him/herself. A man of integrity and talent who made me laugh.

College had already opened up a broader spectrum of life for me and Colin widened that outlook even further. My dad was right when he first saw his photograph and mumbled, 'He's no nine to five man.'

As I struggle to be self-reliant I often wish I'd got my husband's quiet common sense. Sure there were plenty of times when we exasperated one another - but how our partners turn into knights in shining armour when they disappear forever.

It was strange leaving everyone to return to Norwich. I must admit, there's a certain comfort being within the family bosom. Like sinking back into a comfortable cushion. I felt particularly sad as I hugged Pat and my little mum. But I'd been away for too many years.

Driving back was not nearly so bad. Seasoned traveller now, wasn't I? In fact, I quite enjoyed it. I stopped at a Transport Cafe for lunch where a girl ('We don't have no rolls on'y bread and butter') kept shouting things like, 'Number 22, sausage and chips.'

The cottage looked wonderful! Balmy day, birds singing. Carpets two feet thick.

I phoned everyone I could think of.

March 26th: Couldn't stop talking at Cruse. One compassionate carer is lessening her workload because of worsening depression. How can she bear so much of other people's pain?

March 27th: Went to the doctor's. Have actually made a decision! You wouldn't like it, Colin. When we used to talk about the menopause we both agreed I'd cope with it naturally. Well, my love, nature hasn't been doing me any favours lately so now the medics can have a go.

I'd been feeling suicidal too often. Perhaps HRT would help lift my spirits. Before Colin died, I'd bought a book called Menopause Naturally. Its views expressed exactly my own. But this business of being up one minute and then down the pan the next was too exhausting. Now I'd try anything. Apart from Hormone Replacement capsules, I came away from the surgery with Zimovane sleeping tablets as well. That afternoon I visited friends.

'Have a lovely Easter,' they chirped and I put a big smile on my face.

I made two more positive moves. I knew now I needed to be among people so volunteered to serve behind the bar in the small theatre of an Amateur Dramatic group. Secondly I went along to see a private counsellor.

'Try and write down everything as you remember it,' she said.

After I'd talked to her I came away feeling curiously light-headed. I had fish and chips in Asda. It was lovely. I wish I could say the lightness stayed with me when I did my stint at the theatre but just as in the charity shop, everyone knew everyone except me. Someone kept saying 'Shush,' while the play was on. Then in the bar I dropped a glass that shattered it, the "Shusher" and me.

Easter Saturday: When will HRT start working? Phoned everyone. Pat is having the family for Easter, Seán says he's marrying the Greek girl-friend in August and my drains are blocked. Heaved up the manhole cover over drain-run. Revolting. Trawled the stagnant pool down there with a rake and grass-grabber. Large wads of toilet paper and stuff floating about. Back to days of bucket-and-chuckit. Mowed lawn. Legs hurt. I can understand why widows rush into hasty second marriages. Someone to unblock the drains. Nothing and no one can help us. Only ourselves. Forging a new solitary life is the pits.

Easter Sunday: Renounced God. There is nothing now. Worked all day in garden. Fell asleep on settee at 6.00p.m. As I was drifting off I clearly heard a voice say, 'Be very brave.' I don't expect anyone to believe me. But I know it happened.

That night I played the runes again. I picked one out blind. It meant, "Be still. Collect yourself. And wait on the will of heaven."

I had phoned someone in the village to enquire about firms that unblocked drains and the next day, two young farmers from the village, David and John Howard, came to the cottage of their own volition and unblocked them. They wanted no payment. And they hardly knew me.

Their kindness restored hope in me.

Then Paul and Martin arrived unexpectedly. They demolished the now unsafe hen house and fitted a telephone extension. Spirits lifted again.

The switchback of life continued. But I never rejected God like that again.

I can't say any particular incident proved a turning point. But slowly, so very slowly, spaces between the lows would lengthen.

I believe my cries did not go unheard that Easter.

TWENTY

'I like your cottage. But I don't think it's worth what you're asking. Tell you what, I'll swop it for my house and massage your knee into the bargain.'

Showing viewers around the cottage held no fears any more. I just laughed at the cheek of the latest potential buyer, a masseur who lived in a small semi-detached.

'My house is in a very nice area,' he insisted.

Swop it for my cottage? In his dreams.

I went back to Norwich Writers' Circle for the first time in a year. It was like going home.

How'd it go? Want a cup of coffee? sprang to mind when I returned that night to the cottage. But Tamba was there to sniffle a welcome.

I enrolled for a Police Defensive Driving Course. It was cheap, enjoyable and very instructive. The only snag was discovering there'd be an assessment of everyone's driving abilities at the end of the course. I'd chicken out of that one.

At Gateway I met E who had been Headmistress of a school for those with learning disabilities. With her husband she wrote a book on the subject. Then, like Colin, he died from a sudden heart attack. She subsequently married L who was such a help at Gateway and they both became dear friends to me.

One day she said, 'I can't believe it was you who answered our call for voluntary help, because since talking to you I've started writing again.'

I couldn't believe something useful had actually emerged out of my situation.

Is it a sense of insecurity that makes us form cliques? At Cruse it seemed to me everyone had his or her buddies. One day I tagged along with a small group going for a pub-lunch and suddenly I was part of the clique. We had a great meal, conversation - and free puddings that day.

Driving assessment day with the Police drew ever nearer. Don't put yourself through it, my unconscious reasoned; the next minute it was sneering, 'Coward.'

'Don't worry, we'll come with you on a practice drive through the city,' said two friends from Cruse. As I only knew one way in and out of the city I jumped at the chance. Comments flowed freely:

'You're exceeding thirty in a built up area.'

'You swerve at junctions.'

'Don't dodge between lanes.'

And the car was pinking.

Sunday was "test" day. I spent Saturday cleaning the car, only to find her dew-doused the next morning. But eventually I drove a sparkling Orion to Police Headquarters.

'It's too late for that now,' shouted a smart Alec from the class, as I breathed on wing-mirrors.

The highly qualified driver from RoSPA who was to sit beside me looked all of sixteen. I'd expected a burly policeman - but he put me at ease at once. I drove more competently (I think) because of it. I was staggered, and flattered when he asked afterwards, 'Have you thought of

160

training for the Advanced Drivers' test?'

'Me?'

'Certainly. You did very well. I'm impressed.'

Oh, wow, he's lovely, I thought.

After I got over the shock I joined a queue of other drivers who must also have impressed their assessors, because they too were collecting forms for Advanced Driver training.

But then came the real treat. The police took us on demonstration drives in perfectly polished police-cars. To show how it should be done!

'You drive rather fast,' I ventured as we whizzed through winding country lanes.

'All very safe and within speed limits, madam. And you can see the empty road ahead.'

It was a real thrill. I loved it. I'd never dare go this fast I thought. Once we reached the city, though, it was a case of dawdling in lines of traffic. Pedestrians glanced curiously towards our police car carrying three excited chattering women.

Then it was back to dull old basic living. As a born whittler, I felt compelled to learn all I could about the workings of everything in and out of the cottage. Sole responsibility weighed heavy. When the man with the tanker (née, honey-cart) arrived to empty the septic tank I watched the procedure carefully.

'Yew could ha' left it longer than this. 'Taint full yet. Look,' he said.

I stared into the depths of what was mainly mine and felt naked before him.

'You'll feel better next year,' folk assured me.

Rubbish. I still searched for Colin in the smell of his clothes, in minute specks of dust in the corners of his pockets, in whisps of greying hair in his shaver.

When he was alive he was always going on about the comb he'd bought on holiday in Germany: 'I can't find my comb, duck.'

'Use another!'

'I don't want another. I want my comb from Koblenz.'

So when it dropped from behind the mirror after he died, I was in no doubt he'd given it a shove.

I was living in a mystical unreal world most of the time. I'd call, 'Want a cup of coffee, duck?' and then close my eyes and imagine his deep even, 'Please.'

He'd never refused coffee. Could it have contributed to his high blood pressure?

Others have told me how they, too, went on talking to their loved ones. If there is one seed of comfort to be gained from these one-way conversations, I'm all for it.

I got fed up with carrying in hod after hod of coke and chucking it on the boiler, or remaking the fire after it had died. I wrote in my diary: 'Fed up with the bloody boiler. Fed up with only me to talk to. FED UP. Made six pounds of marmalade.'

Well that was a shred of orange light in the darkness if I made marmalade. But I don't suppose I would have thought so then.

Grief can produce a gamut of emotions but I was certainly not prepared to feel as lively as a swallow in summer one morning. Unnaturally so. Was this the effect of HRT? It was great to be fluttering and flying, after having some bleeding and considerable mood swings during the month.

I bounced to the doctor's. He wasn't as happy as me about the high I was on. He changed the prescription to Livial that doesn't involve a bleed. He said there were no side effects... I did get some extra facial hair however and my libido burst forth - not what I was looking for at all! But, more important, I began to feel less depressed and had more energy. That was good.

Bluebell Day and tea serving came around again. One gentle soul with sorrowful eyes, said quietly to me: 'I hear you've had a bit of bad luck.'

There wasn't time to be sad for long though. I was passing the food tent when I spotted Reg a widower whose wife died just before Colin. He was vigorously polishing wineglasses,

'Don't tell me they've let you serve the booze,' I cheeked.

'Just watch your lip,' he retorted.

We were very aware of one another's feelings but acting around and laughing helped a lot.

I was of more use pouring teas than I was with the Amateur Theatre Group. Perhaps it was because of the crashing crockery fiasco they asked me to collect admittance tickets instead of serving behind the bar. A woman in charge bore down upon me:

'Do you realise you've been handing back the wrong half of everyone's ticket? Tchk!'

It seemed I was only functioning in short spurts.

Another kind elderly widower at Cruse asked me to have lunch with him. By this time I'd got over stomach cramps that happened whenever anyone asked me out. Besides he really was a charming and interesting little man. During lunch the conversation turned to the subject of marriage.

'I shall never marry again,' I told him.

'Oh, but you don't know that. You might change your mind,' he said, Death-by-Chocolate Pudding dribbling down the corners of his mouth.

I shook my head.

He sighed, 'It is so difficult getting to know ladies at Cruse. I mean, one can't very well interrupt conversations to go round and interview them.'

Interview? Blimey, I thought. This is my interview.

He drove me home speedily after that, peering short-sightedly into the distance. At one point his car mounted the pavement where a woman wheeling a pram was walking towards us. I vowed I'd never let an old man drive me again. The sooner I took my Advanced Driver's training, the better.

Dealing with practicalities Colin had once attended to, became a necessity. I cut down something in the garden every day to prevent being buried alive. I was always on the watch for trusty workmen who could stop taps dripping or fix gutters. Other times it was make-do-and-mend. When the dog ran into the curtains and broke plastic screws holding the curtain-rail on the wall, miles of sellotape held them firmly together once more.

One day C and I went shopping in a place where shelves were

crammed with crockery.

'Don't swing your handbag,' I muttered.

'Gracious, no.'

The next minute I knocked over a cut-glass bowl. It was like bomb exploding. Everyone around me froze. Everybody stared. C vanished. I stared at fragments of glass at my feet. No use grubbing around for celotape this time. My friend re-appeared, chalky-faced, 'Just keep calm and walk out.'

We walked like zombies towards the door. But my whittling conscience made me collar an assistant and confess what had happened in the belly of the store. He told me not to worry at all, collected a sweeping-brush and cleared the mess. Pleasantly too. The shop was Latham's at Potter Heigham.

I was now meeting a completely new set of people to those Colin and I had known as a couple. The common bond that linked most of us was loss of a loved one. Yet I still had no sense of belonging anywhere. Colin had been my anchor. Compatibility and true happiness when it came bonded us like superglue. Sure it's a cliché, but after he died I did not know who I really was. Perhaps I should have fled back to Cornwall and tried to "find" myself among the artistic brigade. Did suburbia lie dormant inside me or was I destined to live alone in a cottage in the country until I was a doddery old lady, wandering and muttering?

Shopping stopped me thinking too much. I went to buy a dress for Seán's impending wedding. It was like something out of Danse Macabre. I swirled in rose flowered polyester in a John Lewis dressing room. I had not realised how saggy, gaunt and grey I'd grown. Any dress was going to have to work miracles.

No such worries about what to wear at the cottage: boots, jeans and jumpers. I was soon nifty with a rip-hook when nettles reached the eaves. Every part of me ached every night. But working in the garden, though I cursed it between stings and slashings, gave me neither time nor energy to carry on crying. But bouts of depression fluctuated like the weather. Then I'd be on a high for the stupidest reason.

'Excuse me, could you screw this back on for me, please?' I was always accosting customers at garages because the petrol cap on the Orion suddenly wouldn't screw back. Then one day an elderly mechanic at an old type civilised garage where they served you showed me how to manoeuvre it myself. I walked on air for days... until those gasmen came to lay pipes across the fields to Coltishall.

'They'll fold back your water pipe, break it and re-seal it,' I was told. Fold it? Break it?

I tore down the loke to watch every move they made. No wonder my hair was still falling out in clumps enough to stuff a pillow. The only folk without worries are dead I kept telling myself. I still panicked. But when I was sick to my socks of it all I did have the sense to remember a few old relaxation techniques. I also started swimming at the local Aqua Park. Such bliss. Why hadn't I done it before? All my concerns, for the time being floated off under flumes.

Sometimes at work, Colin's telephone had never stopped ringing, everyone expecting priority treatment. When he didn't know which way to turn next, he'd shut the door and close his eyes, trying to achieve a few moments total relaxation.

If you are reading this and you have a partner, cherish that partner. I'd give my all to have a second stab at our life together, a life where Colin might have concentrated more on what he loved doing most, painting. But it's easy isn't it in hindsight? All we do know for sure is we only live once. But, thank God, buying the cottage and living close to nature was one major fulfilment in his life.

I wondered if I'd ever laugh again and mean it, but some sunny moments dribbled along. One warm afternoon we took the group from Gateway to Mousehold Heath where we had a picnic and played rounders. Later we sang to the accompaniment of a guitar. Such peaceful moments remain in the mind.

And I began writing again.

May 25th 1991: My love, you died fifteen months ago exactly. I never cease to love and miss you. I've photocopied tributes to you from friends, all of them exceedingly shocked by your death and am sending them to the boys in sealed envelopes so they can open them when they feel like it. They loved you and I want them to know of the esteem in which others held you. Letters like this:

> Dear June,
>
> At such a time words are so inadequate. I hope you can understand the wealth of feeling for you at this time among those of us at work who enjoyed Colin's wit and wisdom and talent, and his constant friendship. We are all the poorer for his loss, but the richer for having known him. May all your memories, and his nearness even in death sustain you and comfort you.

Bank Holiday Monday: Estate agent phoned. Viewers wanted to see the cottage. Flew round the place cleaning like crazy. No one turned up.

6th June: Treated myself to a full breakfast at BHS for 99p. Better than sitting alone in the cottage.

I was always looking for an escape from myself and my surroundings. One evening Iris and I went to an introductory talk on Transcendental Meditation. Watching slides in the quiet warm room, we both fell asleep. Afterwards we proceeded to the bar and stayed there until closing time. Better than sitting alone in the cottage. I learned nothing about Meditation but was inspired to carry on practising Yoga on the sitting-room carpet. I found it did help me. The mind can't go on whirring when all the muscles are floppy.

'Tell me more about this Livial I'm taking,' I asked my doctor. But it wouldn't have mattered what he said, I'd have carried on taking it. I slept better and had more energy to try activities that would drag me out of my awful depressions.

One task I set myself was to take that RoSPA Advanced Driving Course. I sent off money for the test which, I was told, I would only take when I was considered to be ready. All training would be given free by highly qualified drivers which I thought was excellent.

8th June: Drove to G's house for my first driving session. Lovely girl about twenty-three with amazing knowledge of driving techniques. She said the first run would simply be to assess me. Was determined to show her I wasn't any old idiot as I drove to Potter Heigham. Saw two friends strolling along the pavement: 'I know them!' I called out. It was my first slip of concentration.

On the way back I felt nicely relaxed.

'It's red!' she exclaimed.

They were a tricky set of traffic lights on Thorpe Road. I had my eyes on the second set of red lights where I would turn right, rather than the preceding red ones. Had to slam on the anchors.

G marked up my initial chart. Apparently I have a lot of work ahead. Homework is to read the first chapter of Roadcraft.

When I got home that Sunday I was SHATTERED. But the whole experience had been entirely exhilarating. And I suddenly discovered the one and only activity in life I preferred doing without Colin.

Driving his car.

It was the start of me being at the wheel.

TWENTY-ONE

Not every new experience was as satisfying as the driving lessons. After the ticket-fiasco I was back behind the bar at the theatre group. I was daft expecting to get accepted too soon. I know now that when you go along to a new group there is always a settling-in period when you are on the fringe, pressing your face to the window watching other kids at the party who all know one another. There were even different people at the bar each time I went so I did not establish nice-to-see-you-again relationships.

One evening I was getting on pretty well with another helper until she suddenly scrambled under the bar.

'You're pretty nimble for a pregnant woman,' I said admiringly.

'I'm not pregnant.'

I told myself I'd got enough problems without worrying about daft things I said and bought a pot Buddha to sit on my mantelpiece.

Seán rang from Greece. The Bishop wanted proof he'd been baptised and was not already married.

'If I can't show a certificate I have to be baptised again,' he wailed.

I'd look for it. As for being married already - what he did in his spare time was none of my business.

Neither relaxation techniques nor Buddha could relieve the pain as I sorted through family documents. It happened like that. I'd be cracking along OK then wham! Back into the pit.

I wrote bitterly in my diary: "If God exists, why doesn't He reach out to help me? Ask and you shall not be given."

Of course, the time was coming when gaps between stomach-churning despair would lengthen; when lying-on-the-carpet relaxation moments would help, even if they did cause tears to flow as body defences slackened. But not yet. A desperate diary entry from one sleepless night reads: "This aloneness at the cottage is without precedent. Tomorrow is only darkness... especially if I wake up."

There was a lot to mull over. Where did I buy the obligatory gun-cabinet to store Colin's shotguns? How was I to fix it? And did I really have to fly to Greece? Was there no other way? And... was I the only person on earth who was awake at three in the morning?

At least I was able-bodied. P who lived alone, fell and fractured both wrists. She was so brave I felt ashamed of my moanings.

Marion told me she'd coped well during the first weeks after her husband died because there was so much to do sorting out his affairs but once all that was in order she fell apart.

There is no one way to grieve.

Sheila was waiting for a major operation after losing her partner.

'I wouldn't deliberately do anything to shorten my life, but I hope I don't wake up afterwards,' she told me.

We both decided, yes, it would be dead easy to go that way, but how awful for our family and friends - and what about going on living for our husbands? How did we know there wasn't something in the Master Plan that decreed we were still here for a reason?

'I suppose we have to realise our own value, don't we?' she said.

So small glimmers of rationality in an otherwise irrational period comforted and bolstered us.

It wasn't easy to adjust to our new status in a world geared to pairs. There's a subtle difference about the way you are treated. Jane said to me:

'When I went on holiday on my own, I joined a group of women to go sightseeing. Well, others in the party were pleasant enough, passing the time of day, etcetera - but there was something missing, somehow. Then later in the week, I went sightseeing with a man. There was a striking difference in the attitude of other couples. They really went out of their way to stop and chat, saying things like, 'Ooh, have you tried eating at so and so's? And a lot more. It was so different, June.'

It happens to us all. Widowed friends remarry and if you aren't a couple you aren't invited to their supper dos. It doesn't do to have an odd number. I mean, imagine the havoc a single woman might wreak. And as for being brave enough to invite two single women…

To strike out singly after being one of those pairs for so long, especially for the elderly, takes courage. We need to be bold - not to worry about what people think as we sit alone in Public Places.

It's what we think of ourselves that matters.

I mention my friend M again who has been on two holidays and several courses on her own this year.

'I enjoy my own company - and I enjoy talking to other people on the courses. Lots of them go on their own. I'm going on a Writing course next. Then I'm thinking of joining the University of The Third Age,' she says.

We have to find a way of coping that suits us. Margo had been married several times and hated being single again. So she did something about it. After advertising in a "Partners Column" she met a man who seemed pleasant enough. But she had the feeling he was more interested in her beautiful home than in her.

'He's got to go,' she told me. A few days later after they parted, she phoned me. 'I told him the relationship wasn't working.'

'What did he say?'

'He asked me what sort of house you lived in.'

The widowed are vulnerable.

I longed for Colin's arms around me. I yearned to talk with him, watch TV with him... I even missed the way he'd slope off with a know-what's-going-to-happen-next expression five minutes before the end of a film. Or the way he'd lean across when I was engrossed in a programme and say, 'You've got a little grin on your face.' I missed him painting and me writing and one of us calling, 'Want a cup of coffee, duck?'

It would have been easy to fall into another man's arms for the pure physicality of it; the joy of being warm and wanted. For months after Colin died I was like a zombie and then after taking HRT, strange sexual longings hit me. It was bewildering and miserable. I longed for Colin in bed and asked him to come to me in dreams. He did.

I wrote a story in which I visualised a future where women on HRT pursued men who wanted nothing more than quiet games of bowls.

The answer in my case was to get stuck into writing and gardening. Becoming absorbed in an activity is a palliative for grief and it made me so tired that at the end of the day I only wanted to sleep.

'I believe there are two watersheds in bereavement,' said my widower friend, Tom. 'For me, the first was after two years when the agonising pain became bearable and I began to notice the world around me. After five years, I got the feeling that perhaps I could settle down with some-body else.'

Like Margo, he did marry again and told his children no one was replacing their mother; the new woman was not "instead of" but "as well".

Life has to move on. And since being on my own I have met many people who eventually find they start to enjoy their quiet independence, develop a comfortable routine, do whatever they feel like doing.

'Living alone is not undelightful,' said Jack.

I used to think my isolated position contributed to my misery, but I met others surrounded by shops and people who felt exactly the same. Jean had a large supportive family around her but got extremely depressed. A visit to her doctor and having anti-depressants prescribed helped her enormously.

You can become very touchy at this time. I won a cuddly toy in a raffle and snarled at the person who made the witless comment, 'Now you'll have something to cuddle at night.'

"Tread on egg-shells when you talk to me," should have been hung around my neck. I turned against me and everybody else. No wonder I didn't have a bosom friend.

It slowly dawned on me I was a rotten driver. After Advanced Training sessions I realised how little I knew. For the first time in years I read the Highway Code. After those Sunday sessions, I'd give my instructor a cheery wave and drive with abnormal diligence back to the cottage. Halfway home I'd realise I was just too tired to make it and, once again, would land up slumped in the car outside McDonalds with burger, coffee and hot crunchy apple-pie, gazing with a glazed expression at cars sweeping along the main road. Until I fell asleep.

For the very first time - and it was after such a training session - I was pleased not to be going out the next morning. Pleased to have time to myself. And if anyone had told me I would ever feel like that I'd never have believed it.

'Why do you wear a man's watch?' said a small sweet woman at Gateway.

'Because she hasn't got one of her own, silly,' her friend said.

'When my husband died, I wanted to keep something of his very close to me,' I said.

'Ahhh.' They both put their arms around me with loving concern.

'My Granny died,' said M.

'I am sorry,' I said.

'She had a dog.'

'What sort of dog?'

'A friendly dog.'

P shoved his head inside his pullover and blew a whistle.

Then we had a discussion about death. There was no embarrassment, no messing about searching for correct terms.

People with learning disabilities should be allowed to mourn in their own way, given time to talk about the person they miss. M went on to tell me all about her Gran.

We all have a desperate need to be loved and comforted. When my Headmistress friend, E lost her husband, she said some of her Staff found it difficult to talk to her, even avoided her, but there was no such embarrassment with people in her care with learning disabilities. They simply put their arms around her.

'We are sorry he died, Mrs M... but he's gone to live with Jesus.'

E said we shouldn't shy away from the subject but talk about it when the need arose. She said a big difficulty that cropped up so often after someone died was when the remaining parent could not let go. The disabled son or daughter became a comfort to have around and all attention was concentrated on them. Unfortunately, when that parent died and the child had to be uprooted to totally different surroundings, the culture shock could be enormous.

Another friend, D, had a stepson of forty with learning disability. When she broke the news to him that his father had died and gone to heaven and they wouldn't see him any more, she said she didn't think it sank in properly. She got up in the middle of the night to see him sitting up in bed with his dolly. She spoke to him gently,

'I know you are feeling unhappy because I am and when you go to Day Centre tomorrow it's all right if you want to cry.'

'My dolly's crying,' he said with a tear running down his cheek.

'She'll be better soon. Remember when Auntie died, we got better, didn't we?

The next morning he said anxiously, 'I did say "Goodbye" to Daddy, didn't I?'

'Oh, yes, you did, dear.' (She'd called him down to say "Goodbye" when his Father went in the ambulance).

Before the funeral D took him to the church: 'This is the row where we shall be sitting and Daddy will be in his coffin there - and there will be a lot of people who will come to say "Goodbye" and "Thank you" to Daddy and we shall sing hymns and say prayers.'

'Will there be a Fly-Past?' he asked,

'No, love, I don't think there'll be that.'

She said to me, 'You won't believe it, June, but as we all left the church, a load of planes flew over.'

2nd July 1991: I have been nominated to be a representative of the group on the Cruse committee. Meetings held near Norwich Cathedral in evening. Dislike night driving. Over a year since Colin died and I still can't make up my mind about selling the cottage. At least I still see familiar landmarks.

'Never refuse any invitation,' I was told, so I attended a reunion at a school where I once taught. A colleague approached me with tears in her eyes.

'I was so sorry to hear about Colin.'

Oh, yes? Too busy to even send a card? I thought.

'How are you coping?'

'Fine. Just fine.'

But it was delightful to talk to old pupils and look at photos of their children. And I'm sure it wouldn't have been one of my lot who stuck chewing gum on the bonnet of my car.

7th July: 'How can you possibly have a damp-proof course in an old cottage?' said one surly viewer.

'It was injected.'

'Injected?'

I spent forever showing him all the plugholes to prove it. What are you doing this for? screamed inside me. Tell him to get lost. That you aren't selling after all.

Felt like bawling after he left - not a clue why. Did some writing instead and felt much better.

11th July: Gave a talk in place of Colin at the Townswomen's Guild Group. He was booked with them to talk about Watercolour Painting; mine was about Writing. In heck of a state before I went. Wondered why I'd ever agreed - except I knew why. Hadn't got to let him down. Life going on and all that stuff. Prayed before I went and... I enjoyed the evening! Townswomen's Guild people are so friendly. Even sold some of my books. Back home in the dark I let Tamba out. I thought I was picking up her ball and there in my hand was a lovely big fat toad.

Apart from toads and rabbits in abundance, moles took over the lawn; more molehills than grass. I tried burying empty milk-bottles so the wind whistled across them. Didn't deter Moley for long. Then I dug into the run and buried the musical part of a Christmas card.

Margo called at the cottage.

'I can hear music coming from my lawn,' I said.

'Go on?'

'Come and listen.'

She knelt with her ear to the ground. Her eyes widened. 'My God, I can hear it, too.'

It gave us a good laugh. And Moley vanished as the lawn continued to play "Jingle Bells" for a fortnight.

In bereavement, laughter and tears are the same. S tells the story of shopping with her friend who was also recently widowed. They had a fit of giggles as they staggered along with bags and parcels. Then suddenly and simultaneously they began to sob in the street.

I heard of a bereaved person who would not go in a meeting room at Cruse because she heard someone laughing. Don't be kidded by laughter. Except it is good for us. Peals of mirth can help people survive. Live longer. Not as though I wanted to know anything about that. I wrote: "All that stuff about things getting better in the second year is rubbish." So when I recently read in my 1991 diary, "Had a nice day", I wondered whatever had happened?

I went on to read: "Picked raspberries, washed car, took Tamba a walk, then driving lessons - very winding lanes to Wymondham, then told to get up a really good speed in third before changing up. It was EXHILERATING!"

Getting out of the cottage once a day seems to have been the key for me. One friend went to Safeway in Cromer every day simply to see other folk. Now she is on so many committees she hardly has time for shopping.

Being active however, did not always lift my despondency. One day I spent ages on top of a ladder repairing plastic guttering with black gooey compound, only for the gutter to break apart again. I was so fed-up. At that moment a friend rang to recount exciting news that he'd been so well paid for a series of newspaper articles he'd taken his large family, including grandchildren, on holiday with the proceeds.

I let the gutter hang and went back to writing.

30th July: Swung from top of ladder to cut overgrown Cupressus hedge with secateurs and fell into nettles. Damn raspberries won't stop ripening. Just go on and on. Had another go at gutter. Climbed into bed well greased with vaseline.

6th August: How could I not find Stratton Hill beautiful? Such boggin' colours. Golden fields swollen with hay bales; sky-blue loaders; scarlet tractors - sunset merging from pearl-pink into orange. Helpers harvesting the fields. Laughing. How privileged we are to be alive.

Pat sent me a huge soft toy - a cuddly brown bear into whose fur I shed my tears. Childlike is what I was and wanted to be. I was glad to know I was not the only one. Maureen said she often cuddled soft toys while Jan's granddaughter lent her a cuddly lion.

'Let me have it back, won't you, Grandma; I'll buy you one for your birthday.'

Well, it was better to cuddle a toy than huddle close to a stranger in a bus as one of my friends did.

I was always re-arranging furniture and sorted out a lot of junk which Iris and I took to a boot sale. I should have hung on a while because later I discovered it was not so junky. Never mind it was a lovely sunny day and we really enjoyed ourselves - and cleared £12 each.

I had the gutter repaired professionally.

8th August: Intensely blue sky. Trees fretworked against bubbly clouds. My uncle had one word to describe everything beautiful: awe-inspiring. The countryside around the cottage - not counting my scruffy garden - is truly awe-inspiring. A Greek poet, Sycladianus, wrote:

It is as if the dead have come alive again,
As if they embraced me
So deep in the ground do our roots mingle
So high are our branches raised in the sky.

How can Colin not be here at Stratton?

Those not-so-dark periods helped me to claw through desolate days when they returned. I still stubbornly refused to succumb to anti-depressants but the time came when they did help me.

I was a bag of nerves about flying to Greece for Seán's wedding. I bought a relaxation tape to listen to soothing sounds on the plane. Too late, I realised it consisted mainly of trickling water!

I was conscious I was going to the wedding representing both Colin and me. How we would all miss him.

I couldn't even begin to take his place.

24th August: I can't go through with it. I'm not going.

TWENTY-TWO

26th August 1991: Of course I'm going. I have to, don't I? And what an effort. Can't believe I've actually finished packing: large suitcase, hand luggage, shopping bag, enormous handbag... all bulging. Dead tired.

Later: Caught 6.55 am. train. Tube to Heathrow. Moving Walkway. All strange and exciting.

£1.25 for an Espresso coffee!

At Heathrow my heart soared as I spotted Paul and Martin swinging guitars at the top of the stairs. Cream-clad and Panama-hatted - straight out of the Mafia.

I'd only been in an airport once - at Norwich when I researched my serial, Flying High, for D C Thomson. Cosy place, Norwich Airport. Noise and bustle at Heathrow left me staring. So did Customs. After a searching look at the boys, our cases were dissected. We all craned necks as Paul's belongings were unfolded.

'String vest?' I said.

He made a wry remark that reminded me of his Father.

I'd packed everything I thought I wouldn't get outside England. Customs plucked out my pills and potions well wrapped in foil and plastic.

'Mum… What have you got there?' Julie whispered hoarsely as Customs picked at the foil.

Once that rigmarole was behind us, it was off to the Departure Lounge. No way would all those people get on one plane I thought. My knees shook.

We sat at the front end of a 262 Olympic Airways plane. As it taxied across the Runway I was torn between shutting my eyes tightly or staring through the tiny windows. With amazing acceleration that made me squeeze my knees together, we shot sky-high. Below wound the Thames. Straight out of Eastenders. Then even higher.

'Look Mum. We're above the clouds. Are you looking?' Martin tapped me on the shoulder.

So this was heaven?

'Are you OK?' Paul turned in his seat in front of me.

A steward appeared with champagne. I don't know whose brilliant idea it was, but it worked. Then more drinks and trays of multi-coloured food. We flew over France, fields, Alps… so… "awe-inspiring". I was dying to go to the lavatory but was afraid to miss something. I had to eventually - splashing their Armani cologne about vigorously.

Huge ochre-coloured craters and mountains rose to meet us. We flew so low I thought we'd land on Athens golf course. I wrote in my diary: 'I don't ever remember such an exciting, thrilling and wonderful experience in my entire life.'

We stepped outside into an oven. No problems going through Greek Customs. Looked honest enough to them, didn't we? Then straight into the arms of my dear Seán.

I stayed with Seán's mother-in-law-to-be, Maria. Neither of us understood the other's language. We spent our time smiling and gesturing. After the silent cottage I loved listening to sounds drifting through shutters: chattering on balconies; priests' chanting through the hot busy air;

the hum and horns of cars.

30th August: Seán's Stag night last night. Dreaded to think what his brothers might do to him. I had to stop myself sneaking after them. The girls took me out on the town. All I remember is drinking beer and brandies and eating chocolate and banana Crepes before going to bed after three a.m. - long before they did. Time seems to mean nothing in Greece. Everyone is late for appointments. Even the clock in the square doesn't work. Martin has graduated from sun-bloc 8 to fast tan oil. Paul says when he swims he leaves an oil slick. I'm on sun-bloc 24. Martin said, 'I want to know where the Greeks get their padded trunks.'

Colin's sister Audrey and husband David were driving across Greece to the wedding and stopped at red traffic-lights only to be deafened by a barrage of road-rage hooting from irate Greek drivers behind them.

As the family relaxed together in sunny squares, joking, drinking coffee and sipping from tall glasses of water, we were not to know that David, too, would be dead the following year.

None of us knows what lies ahead (but what laughs we had, David).

On the day of the wedding, dark-haired, fashion-conscious brides-maids in their own choice of short dresses, filled Maria's house waiting for the hairdresser and beautician. The latter arrived and after everyone smiled and gestured in my direction, she touched my face with her dainty finger. I was flattered by her obvious approval. I had spent forever on my make-up. She whipped out her bag, wiped my face clean and began to pamper and pat me with super subtle eyeshadows, palest pink lipsticks and mascara - which I'd never worn. What a transformation. I've never been able to repeat the effect.

Seán and I were to drive together to the outdoor ceremony. Before leaving, he and I stood alone on the balcony of his flat in the balmy Greek air. How I longed to say something appropriate yet witty to him like Colin would have said. There'd always been a good rapport between the two of them. They'd driven to work together, gossiped, enjoyed the same dry sense of humour and bright intellect. Where Colin painted, Seán read avidly and was a talented writer.

Once, after he'd spent time at home from college helping Colin lay a patio, Colin said to me, 'He always asks if there is anything I'd like him to do before he goes back. I like that.'

After Colin died, Seán once said to me, 'When I think about Dad, I don't know whether to laugh or cry.'

I can see Colin grin at that - just as Seán suddenly did on that hot day in Greece. Looking immaculate in a cream suit, he suddenly took out his thin gold spectacles and held them up. They only had one arm. I remembered Colin playing the fool, rolling off the settee and breaking his glasses and wearing them at a ridiculous angle afterwards. How we had all laughed.

It was our memory to hold on to.

On his wedding day.

I was determined not to cry at the ceremony. I didn't. Partly because I did not understand what the grey-bearded, pigtailed priest was saying as he circled a table, leading a small dark Greek girl and a tall slim fair-haired man.

I stood outside myself watching them, my hand sticky with almonds and daisy-petals before we pelted the happy couple.

The blocking out of reality stayed with me late into the night, all through the festivities and dancing.

Until the next morning.

Up to then I had been forcing myself to be jolly and strong and not to dwell on Colin's absence. But alone in my room with the Wedding over, I wept.

There is a language that is universal to all women. Maria entered my room. I could only point to Colin's photograph. She put her arms tightly around me and, in broken English, she said,

'I-love-you.'

TWENTY-THREE

Slapping paint around is enormously therapeutic. I'd recommend it, regardless of the results.

Back home at the cottage and feeling worldly wise I got stuck into decorating. I read that preparation was everything so I scrubbed and scraped, using backs of spoons and a baking-bowl spatula for poly-filling.

I asked John, who'd done our brickwork, if he would repoint the small back chimney. He did, but refused to take any money, saying, 'Colin was very good to me.'

It's what everyone said.

3rd October 1991: Rang the accountant. He still hasn't done anything about the tax-form I sent him in May. His smiling voice said: 'Yours is the very next one I'm doing. I've got it right in front of me now.'

5th October: Had a horrible dream. Was angry with Colin because he put his arms around me and I couldn't feel them.

6th October: I'm giving up this Advanced Driving lark. It's too difficult. Too much to learn. I don't want to be tested on the stupid Highway Code.

15th October: Painted the bathroom pink. Colin hated pink. I don't give a damn, Colin. I like it.

Sunday: Went to Church. I'm going off Church people. Only the Vicar seems genuinely friendly. Back home I slashed nettles down. Knee hurts. So do I.

22nd October: Ford garage in Norwich held a Women's Workshop… showed us bits under the bonnet and how to change a wheel etcetera. It was brilliant. Afterwards there was a video about safety for women-drivers, followed by a marvellous buffet. And all free. On the way home I told Colin how much I enjoyed driving his car. I do. I love it. Changed my mind about the test. I am going to read up on everything. Especially the Highway Code.

27th October 1991: Today would have been the big 60 for you, my love. Bought a bottle of whisky to toast you. Forced it down. How I miss cuddling you. How I miss your touch, your gentleness, your quiet even voice… even your cynicism. How I do so miss your manliness.

An elderly man asked me out for dinner and even braved the loke to call for me in his car.

'I've forgotten something,' he said. 'I have to stop at my house on the way.' I sat in the car wondering what it was. A little posy perhaps? He came out of his house puffing.

'Forgot my teeth-fixative,' he said. And beamed brightly.

I dreamed Colin and I went shopping together; he put his briefcase down and was not at all bothered when it disappeared. Did it mean he was happy to be free of all the worry?

My driving tutor arranged for me to have a session with a top RoSPA trainer. First, he scribbled notes, then we stopped for a while to talk about my faults. Secondly, he went on to instruct me: I was to drive faster... it would make me think quicker:

'Observe well ahead; brake firmly; accelerate smoothly...'

His general comments written at the end of the Assessment Form were:

"Scared of the unknown therefore is being over-cautious but can do it when shown all the advantages of the road ahead."

Story of my life!

4th November: Told the blooming accountant I hoped he'd sent my tax forms in by now. He assured me, 'I've got them in front of me right now. I shall be doing yours next.' I haven't had an accountant before and if this is what happens I won't have another. Would he have messed me about like this if I'd been a man? Woke in the night worrying.

5th November: Two men came to lop the Cupressus trees. One knocked at the door with a bunch of flowers: 'I thought you might like these from my garden, Ma'am. They'll only get blown over in the wind.' It was kind and lifted my spirits. I keep dreaming about Colin. He kissed me. I cried. He said, 'What's the matter?' I said, 'I didn't think we'd be able to kiss any more.' He said, 'I'll put them in a box for you and you can take one out whenever you want.' It was such a "Colin" remark. I walked to the village hoping I might see someone to talk to. I glimpsed a couple washing-up in their well-lit kitchen. Cosy enough to cry for. Know-all friend said I have to let go of Colin. Twit.

7th November: Visited Tax Information Centre in Norwich to try and sort out this tax business. Very helpful, reckon I can do it myself. Felt stupidly lonely in City even after all this time. Called at Cruse but felt strangely lonely there as well. Must be something wrong with me.

This time it was physical. I began bleeding. The doctor prescribed tablets to cause a once-and-for-all final bleeding. I wondered if this was the best time to do it because I felt awfully depressed anyway. He suggested anti-depressants. Back home I cleaned my Study. For saying I'd done so little writing, the place was a tip. I knew I had to get my life in some sort of order. I had to write seriously again. I began with a snotty letter to the accountant.

12th November: Read Desmond Morris in the Daily Mail - that an ounce of anxiety will always do more damage to your body than a pound of fat.

Cut the Cupressus hedge with my nice new secateurs. God knows why we planted stupid Cupressus trees.

For the first two years after Colin died I was like a child, looking to others for guidance. But then hadn't I always done so? My father had dominated my childhood and beyond. Later, I relied very much on Colin. Now, I had to search out my own self from somewhere, however distorted its image.

Learning to rely on my own judgement, believe in myself was difficult. I have more confidence now but occasionally an outward show of belligerence hides insecurities.

With Dad training me, I had become the Northern Counties' Sprint Champion at seventeen because I was fast. Now I had to learn not to rush. When the video went wrong again I learned not to jab frantically at every button but slow down and read the instruction manual carefully. I found I was capable of being methodical after all and "Whooped" every time I fixed it.

But there was nothing steady or methodical about bereavement. I was still either on a false high or stumbling blind in a pit. I could laugh or cry between blinking.

I accompanied my elderly friend to a play production at a local school. Afterwards, he took a wrong turning in the dark. Trailed by other cars we were all soon cruising around the school Netball pitch.

'How on earth do we get out?' he said savagely.

As we reached the tail of following cars to complete the circle I cracked up. But he didn't think it was at all funny: 'Look for the gate!' he barked.

I could not see anything through streaming tears of laughter. Control snapped. We were circling forever round that pitch.

But I was not laughing the next day when I rang my accountant.

'I've had an estimated assessment from the Income Tax office. I owe them £1400! Didn't you send them my tax form?' I yelled.

'It's quite normal to get an assessment. Don't worry. I'll sort that out,' he said calmly.

'I don't want you to do it for me any more! And I'm not going to pay you either!'

14th December 1991: Fog envelops fields outside. The only person I spoke to today was widower friend, Wally who appeared through the mist like Santa Claus, carrying a Christmas card. Cheers Wally. Tonight I'm in a dream-state. Family memories won't go away. Must stop this. Activity! Make cup of tea. Ghosts still won't shift. Face it... no one can help me. Only I can help me. Only I am in charge of my life. Part of me wants to die. Part of me knows I must live. Because I have promised Colin the gift of living for both of us. He gave me thirty-five precious years. Thank God we always said, 'I love you.' Because on that terribleday he died we didn't have the chance.

Reading my diary now, I remember how it gave me strength to write like this. Soul-clearing if you like.

17th December: Our Wedding Anniversary. Thick foggy morning. I stared through the kitchen window. Gradually a faint watery sun began to expand through the clouds. Its outer ring grew brighter until a massive circle of light exploded through the gloom.

It was like the most beautiful present.

That evening the phone crackled annoyingly. My hip was hurting so I took two painkillers and went to bed. At five am the bedside phone rang:

'Hello... Mrs Sutton...?'

'Who is it? Can't hear you very well... interference...?'

'The police are outside your cottage.'

Did I go out with my hands up?

'Your panic-button has gone off in the police-station.'

'I haven't touched it!'

I staggered downstairs, tatty and drawn in a torn dressing gown. A handsome hunk of policeman appeared in the porch in a halo of flashing blue light.

'Have you got your identity-card?' I asked when he wanted to come in.

'It's a long time since anyone asked me for that.' He produced it with a grin.

He'd already walked all round outside the cottage and the dog had not stirred. It seemed broken telephone lines had activated the alarm.

But it was lovely to have someone to talk to (I'd ditch that dressing gown).

TWENTY-FOUR

I don't know any bereaved person who looks forward to Christmas. And only those who have lost a partner and live alone will fully understand, so I won't bother to explain.

I certainly wanted the Festive Season over quickly... and I have always loved Christmas, from first fond memories of Grandma's parties when her family of ten children, plus kids, bombed into her plump-cushioned, piano-thumped, paper-garlanded home.

It's easy to say we must not feel sorry for ourselves. But we do. Isolation and loneliness exacerbate despair. Especially when we are hammered on all sides by happy-family media hype. One friend closed her mind to Christmas, stocking up on favourite magazines instead. Beryl helped serve festive meals to old people locally. Me? I caught a train to Derby again. Couldn't contemplate being alone at Christmas, could I? Crikey. No people? ... It was to be many years before I became even moderately self-sufficient.

Don't be fooled by the apparently self-sufficient. When I attended a dear friend's funeral mourners packed the village Church. All of us were shocked and saddened by his departure. But he'd spent the previous Christmas alone.

Where were we all then?

When he collapsed on his own at home, no one realised. The police gained entrance after forty-eight hours. Since this has happened, several of us have made sure someone trustworthy has access to our door keys and we also have telephone numbers handy.

23rd December 1991: Desolate when I eyed the case I'd packed for one. Rang friend for mutual support. She said sadly, 'Something urged me to visit my husband's grave. I took some holly. But when I got there I realised what a poor specimen it was. It didn't even have any berries on it. Only a red bow. And that was torn. So I took it home again.

'Do you think there'll ever be a time when it doesn't hurt?' she said.

Paul sent me a kilogram of sugared almonds. I got through a lot of them while trying to forget.

Our own pain blinds us from seeing how tortuous it is for those who love us and try to help. Pat and Ken were marvellous to me each Christmas. There are such saints in families.

Back home I got stuck into DIY. After calibrating a gadget for detecting electric wires in walls, I attempted to put up a paper-towel holder. Screws continually fell out of holes I'd drilled in the thick kitchen walls. I needed Rawlplugs which I'd never used. I rang my long-suffering brother-in-law.

'It says to use a drill No. 12 and screws 6-12. How do you tell the size of a screw?'

Had I used a masonry-drill? No, I hadn't. (So I probably ruined the drill I'd used.)

'I suggest you use a No. 8 screw and take into account the width of the towel-holder and half an inch for plaster before you reach brick,' he suggested.

That afternoon Peggy and I sashayed around a DIY store. I found an assistant: 'Screws for a brick wall, please - and what does counter-sunk cross head mean?'

'It means the heads don't stand proud,' she said.

Peggy, an elegant widow who looked as if she had never wielded a tack-hammer in her life declared, 'I know that.'

And the prices! Rawlplugs £2 a packet! (Colin had paid 55p). And £2.29 for one little drill. I spread nails, screws, drills and screwdrivers on the kitchen table. After noting a little picture of a tiny hammer on Colin's Black and Decker, I drilled warily. It worried me when red brick-dust puffed out. Those walls had been there over a hundred years. Suppose I did something awful to them? Colin's walls.

I felt nothing but pure delight when my Rawlplugs fitted my holes so snugly. Would the screws fit? The first one went in fine. The second was at an angle. But it went in. I'd fixed my first gadget.

I skipped. I sang. I was elated.

You could swing on that holder and it wouldn't move. Admittedly a paper towel hides unseemly scratches, but nevertheless, what a master-piece!

29th December 1991: Fell asleep after lunch. Dreamed, oddly, that I had one leg in Colin's trousers and his leg was in there, too. Lit a candle to him. Received letter from accountant. Notice of impending Court procedure if I don't pay his bill. Stuff him. Went shopping and bought a dress, make-up and putty. Wonder what Colin would say if he knew I'd stayed here this long on my own. Does he rest easy? I want him to rest but keep calling him back. In another dream, I said to him, 'Show me how to do that in case you drop dead.' He looked hurt and I exclaimed, 'Well, you did it once!' Then I woke up and wished I hadn't said it.

The following Monday I drove into Norwich, made a cock-up of driving into the car park and realised my RoSPA trainer was following in her car. I walked around the City feeling fed up with continued loneli-ness (before Colin died I'd never been lonely before in my life). It was no good waiting for anyone to drive down my disgusting loke to visit me. No good expecting anyone to visit me, period. I had to get my finger out and do something positive if I wanted things to change.

On sudden impulse I went into Eastern Counties Newspaper Offices and put an advert. in the local paper:

Widow wishes to meet other widowed people in the Aylsham area with a view to starting a social/support group.

Someone once said impulses come from the devil. Oh, my God, I suddenly thought. What have I been and gone and done?

January 1992: A New Year. Surely it can only get better? Nearly two years in hell without Colin. A pane of glass broke in the front door. My stomach knots when something breaks or goes wrong.

I took measurements for a new piece to the glazier, in both inches and centimetres.

'You just do it in inches next time, dear,' he patronised.

I'm good at measuring… but he cut it to the size he thought anyway.

While I was shopping for panel-pins I realised with a pleasant mini shock I was capable of fixing shelves or anything else now if I wanted.

It was great when Martin arrived; he fixed my bicycle-seat and chipped old putty from the door. I was glad he did that. Bum job. The glazier had cut the sheet of glass too small. Knew it! Took it back. He cut it to my correct measurements and I fixed it. Never mind that the putty was finger-print-potholed… it was in! (You can overwork putty; there comes a time when you have to leave it.)

A chisel is like a screwdriver but bevelled at the sides, and it's very very sharp. Unfortunately had a go at a screw with one.

10th January 1992: Received six letters in reply to advert about starting a club for the widowed, mainly from Cromer direction. The Press want to do story on it. Don't know about that. Phoned Vicar in next village to ask if I could talk to him (it would be a change for him to see me not in tears). He arrived on the doorstep clutching his Bible (business card?). He is so dishy, I can't understand why he's not been snapped up. He was thrilled with the idea of a club for the widowed; said he knew of a small chapel I might be able to use and would put me in touch with the

Minister. Then he gave me a hug (mind, he hugs everybody). It's nice though. My mind whizzed back to when Colin used to kiss me before he left for work and sometimes I'd give him an intimate squeeze. He'd laugh and say, 'One day you'll forget and do that to the Vicar!'

I needed to sort out the order of priorities for this proposed club. Transport in rural areas is a problem. It could be overcome if we shared cars.

Sunday: Thought I ought to show up at Church, the Vicar being so helpful and that. I was fine in the Family Service bit when the children sang but was a wimp in the serious grown-up part... I don't know what I believe any more. Mind in chaos about God and the Church. I'm going to see how many days I can last without crying.

24th January: Seán rang. He's dubbing the voice of a gay Polish cavalry officer in a Greek film about Lord Byron. A far cry from being an ant in Thorpe Grammar School play.

I asked his wife (now ex.) how things were going with her school and she replied, 'Very well, but alas, my English master has escaped.'

25th January: Booked chapel in Aylsham for first meeting of widows and widowers.

28th January: Took posters round Aylsham. Butcher said, 'Is it a Dating Agency?'

29th January: Press-photographer came to cottage. Liked him immediately, an artist who, like Colin, had trained at Guildford.

I received a leaflet about the Writers' Summer School at Swanwick in Derbyshire. Colin had once said. 'It sounds really good. I think you would enjoy it.'

In the City I overheard a woman say, 'I decorated my bathroom and John said to me, "You've done Dad proud, Mum."' I thought how much I'd love someone to say to me, 'You've done Colin proud.'

12th February 1992: First meeting of widows' and widowers' group. I was extremely nervous. Peggy and I arrived two hours early to put heating on. 'How many cups shall we put out?' Peggy said. 'Twelve to be on the safe side,' I said. 'What about meeting in this little kitchen? It's cosier in here.' Thirty-five folk turned up. If this gets off the ground, perhaps I shall feel that not all is total waste. A sad man who'd cared for his wife before she died said he was not going to offer to do anything because he was just getting back into the social swing. Others, shy and nervous - and mostly coming on their own - were talking together. It was brilliant to have company. I'd love this club to be a friendly welcoming place for those of us who are alone.

At that first meeting we sat in a circle in the main room and chatted about what sort of club we wanted. It was probably the only afternoon we met when you could hear yourself speak because as soon as people got to know one another there was always a great din.

It transpired everyone hated Sundays. Why didn't we arrange to go out for pub-lunches together? Why didn't we meet twice a month and have speakers? Or simply meet and talk together? Talk. That was important.

There was a great mix. One lady had lost her husband three months previously after fifty years of marriage. Another, many years before. I soon discovered my own feelings were not at all unique. Everyone there had experienced great loss, sadness and pain and yet before the end of the meeting there was much chat and laughter.

It had to keep going!

A week later a widow rang me in tears. She had heard about the group and simply wanted to talk to me. Her husband had just died and she was desolate. I remembered how much I, too, had needed a voice on the end of a phone. I gave her Cruse's number. She contacted them, then came to us at a later stage.

The second meeting at the chapel was far more relaxed with people talking non-stop and with gusto. Wally from the nearby village of Buxton gave a funny talk (to be one of many) about a chicken he knew. He made us all laugh. Some may have arrived close to tears but left, smiling.

We coerced, pushed and persuaded a Committee to come together. Facing it Together was born.

TWENTY-FIVE

The club was going to transform our lives… but healing would still take its own time

25th February 1992: The second anniversary of Colin's death. If Jesus is alive in spirit then Colin is alive as well. Do I pray to one and chat to the other? Such a muddle I'm in. Am I in love with a ghost? I know nothing will ever be the same again, look the same, feel the same. Everyone tries to persuade me to leave the cottage but Colin is so close to me here. I can still hear him saying, 'I'll build you a home you'll love.' I can't cope with the blasted garden, Colin. That's a wilderness like me. If I had one wish, apart from the obvious, I would wish for crystal-clear thinking, to know what step to take next. Cruse suggests you don't make any big decisions for a year after bereavement. Only one year? … There was hardly a day in thirty-five years, my love, when we did not touch. Now I feel like an addict with withdrawal symptoms. I see you in the garden walking towards me in the sunshine with your lovely half shy smile. I dance around the kitchen imagining I am dancing with you. OK, so dancing wasn't your thing and you'd do the Sutton Shuffle instead - but I don't care. Being close to you is what I imagine... This morning I fell asleep on the settee wondering what it would be like not to wake up. Why does my will to live seem to be getting more frail? It frightens me because I know I am becoming the worst sort of coward. You'd be horrified at the thought of throwing away a life... But, duck, I'm so sick and bloody tired of continually having to give myself pep talks. Too hard. And I'm too sad.

That afternoon I had to force myself to go to Gateway. They were all singing with percussion instruments - songs like, She'll Be Coming Round The Mountain When She Comes. I sat with little Yvonne and she laughed when I forgot the words.

Thank God I had the sense to get out of the cottage again.

I didn't give myself a verbal telling off for my bout of the miseries but I wrote a sort of prayer in capital letters on a large piece of cardboard to instil it into my brain:

THIS IS THE HARDEST RACE OF MY LIFE. FINISHING THIS RACE IS WORSE THAN ANY I REMEMBER AS A YOUNG SPRINTER. IF THERE IS A POWER IN THE WORLD AND IF ANYONE IS LISTENING TO ME, GIVE ME BACK THE WILL TO LIVE. GIVE ME THE COURAGE.

When Martin invited me to one of his gigs in London I knew I must accept. I was the oldest swinger there. But it was dark, thankfully. His mates stamped and clapped as he played guitar and sang his own brilliant songs. There was a really nice crowd and soon everyone was dancing. All eyes swung towards Paul when he entered the room. That was no surprise - he looked like his father. He asked me if I'd like to dance and I did. A memory to treasure. Then Mart. said,

'The last song is for my Mum.'

It was a lovely evening.

27th February: The silly Insurance company won't insure my car because I write fiction! They say it would be different if I were a technical writer. Why? I asked. Did they think I was at risk of romancing the stone?

28th February: Since advertising F.I.T. people have been ringing me, often in tears. So many lonely unhappy people out there. How dare I wallow in self-pity?

F.I.T. met twice monthly in the chapel with speakers and social events. One man wanted to learn how to make pastry like his wife did it; women needed DIY tips. A surveyor talked to us about the workings of our houses and told us how to climb into the attic safely and waggle the ball cock in the water tank if it stuck and water overflowed. I did and discovered my ballcock needed replacing.

It's sensible to have a loft-ladder and a mobile phone to carry around because when I climbed up there I couldn't get down again. I panicked and slithered on my stomach across horrible glass-fibre wadding between the rafters, until I could wiggle my feet back on the ladder I'd lodged in the opening. At one time it would have been easy-peasy but after Colin's death, arthritis took hold with a vengeance.

So sort out loft accessibility before you have to go poking around up there.

F.I.T. was a wonderful way of meeting new people… many who'd suffered, more than you. There were so many mourning loved ones; so many achingly lonely. It helped no end when we went for Sunday pub-lunches together (Sunday can be the pits).

At some Wednesday meetings we had group activities; we played Scrabble; one man led a sketching group, Daphne led handicraft and another demonstrated the awkward business, or so I thought then - (done loads since) - of changing a plug.

Lately, a group of us have entered for pub quizzes. And every Christmas we afford a coach to collect members for a splash Christmas lunch - to say nothing of our very professional Christmas concert performances!

I love the din of conversation and not being able to get a word in.

Like Jeanette said, 'It's awful living alone when you're a talker.' And people are so mindful and caring. One newly bereaved woman entered the hall for the first time and a member who had never met her, walked across, arms outstretched, and hugged her.

There were many more women than men. I missed men's company… nothing to do with sex; at that time the thought of making love to anyone other than Colin was abhorrent to me… but masculine chat. So I did something I had never done in my life:

"Widow who prefers creative pursuits and interesting conversation to housework would like to meet gentleman."

The big mistake was admitting to not liking housework. Housework and the enjoyment of same are synonymous with caring. There's the saying: "A woman wants a purse and a man wants a nurse."

One friend, who advertised herself as a solvent widow, received nearly eighty replies to her advert. And she went on to remarry. I received two replies to mine and didn't. I phoned the man whose letter was decipherable. Instead of sounding intelligent, I became a nervous jabbering mass. We arranged to meet for coffee in a local pub.

As the date drew nearer, I panicked. I knew nothing about this man. What had I done? I felt I'd hit the depths and confided in a friend in case I got shipped out to the casbah.

'Don't be daft,' she said, 'you've done the right thing meeting in a public place - and you would be surprised how many of us do advertise for partners.'

'I don't want a partner. Just male company sometimes.'

'You miss Colin.'

I arrived at the pub first and hid behind some bushes. A man about my height arrived. He turned out to be an armchair philosopher with teeth and hands like spades. He bought me a coffee and I sat listening to him for an hour. I bought him a coffee and listened to him for another hour. He asked me nothing about myself. Perhaps it was his way of being tactful. The aroma of lunches being cooked became overpowering. We left to the scowls of the landlord.

This was a long time ago. If it happened now, things would be different. I'd certainly buy myself some lunch whether he wanted any or not.

I landed back at the cottage with an immense feeling of relief and vowed I would never do anything like that again. That night I dreamed Colin and I were walking peacefully together along a glass-sided corridor, watching folk scuttling like ants outside. I said, 'Nothing is important, is it?' Then I remembered he was dead and asked him to hold me very tight.

From then on, enjoyable events began to happen. Everyone from F.I.T came down my loke to a coffee-morning. Reg from the next village cycled.

'Not ruining my car on that blooming track of yours,' he said.

'You're all right if you stick to five miles an hour,' I said.

'Don't know what possesses anybody to live down here,' he said. I couldn't understand why he thought that.

We all shouted him down.

It was arranged for a group of us wanna-be advanced drivers to go on the skidpan at Fakenham. An instructor drove us three at a time between strategically spaced tyres. Then we each had a go at the wheel. I loved it! Marvellous! And it gave us more confidence to deal with emergencies on the road.

When I'm driving in my basic car I try to remember that a front-wheel skid is often caused by excessive speed for the road or weather conditions. To remove the cause I

a) release the accelerator

or

b) declutch and release the accelerator.

I then steer gently into the skid.

All actions must be done smoothly. Nothing harsh.

The book "Roadcraft" has a detailed chapter on skidding. I also received very helpful information from the Institute of Advanced Motorists.

After the enjoyable morning skidding, I treated myself to lunch at the Old Mill Restaurant. The food was splendid but I was the only person sitting alone in a full room.

When I returned home I heard my friend's beloved teenage son had been killed that day in his car.

Fun and frolics were forgotten.

No one knows what lies around life's corners.

7th April 1992: Plastered and painted all day. Spoke to no one. I bet all my folks think I'm OK now. Shall I go back for counselling?

'We didn't have counselling years ago and we got through,' I hear people say. Goody for them.

I didn't consider acquaintances who vanished after Colin died, as friends. One sent me a bunch of flowers after the funeral and I didn't hear from her again. I heard from her husband though. He rang to ask me to join them for a pub-lunch. I almost accepted but in the middle of his conversation he exclaimed, 'Have to go - the wife has just come in.'

Wise widows only accept invitations from the wife.

8th April 1992: I am most unable to cope when not feeling well or I'm tired. Told E how I felt.

'What about your writing?' she said. 'You've got to keep writing.'

'It's crap,' I said.

'Colin wouldn't like to hear you say that,' she said severely.

He was getting at me through her.

9th April: So many heavy buckets of coal and coke. Hip hurts. Why ever did we have such big rooms to decorate and big lawns to cut? Fool me! How am I expected to write when I've got so much else to do? How did Colin fit it all in?

Acute despondency was mirrored in dreams. Colin wanted to get up early to walk across the fields. I did not want him to go without me and I punched him.

10th April 1992: B said, 'You ought to make a concerted effort to sell the cottage.' I don't like anyone telling me what to do. No one knows what it is like in my shoes so no one is in a position to give advice. This is my home. My cottage. I'll sell when I'm ready and not before.

How angry I was becoming again. No, it was not the right time to make decisions. But what a misery I was turning into.

20th April: Oh, what a lovely Easter. I don't believe it. The weather is perfect. Eight of us from F.I.T. went for a pub-lunch and then on to Anne's cottage for cups of tea and a chat. Sitting in a house full of people talking and laughing instead of sitting alone was wonderful.

Facing It Together became a very important part of my life: going places, doing things. With others who understood. One member said to me, 'This club has given me something to live for.'

There were differences of opinion just as there are in families. After our first pub lunch, the men were all for paying by one cheque - everyone paying the same amount regardless of what was eaten.

'But I didn't have coffee or pudding,' exclaimed some of the women. So a long queue formed as members paid individually with the men red-faced and muttering. How we have changed. We now have a favourite hotel where we pay by club cheque. And everybody chokes everything down.

Don't say women are not flexible.

My life was still made up of everlasting lists with scraps of sticky paper slapped all over the kitchen: reasons to move house; reasons to stay; how much to move...? For the same amount I could get someone to do all my repairs and mow the lawn forever.

Even if I did move, I did not know where I wanted to live. And I knew I'd feel guilty about leaving our lovely cottage, built with sweat and tears - and a plaque over the door, too. I loved it. It was a home worth handing down to descendants (health and old persons' home permit-ting!) Where grandchildren could taste country living and play in grassy corners.

Oh guilt! The bete-noire of bereavement. Why do we hurt ourselves? To take on a smidgen of the pain he/she suffered?

But, slowly, it began to sink in, there was something else keeping me at the cottage.

April: Tonight I gardened. It was the most beautiful still evening. I heard the first cuckoo. Curls of smoke swung softly from the boiler chimney across an apricot sky. Such peace.

How can I possibly leave this place?

TWENTY-SIX

2nd May 1992: I continue to toss the ball of indecisiveness about… If I don't move to where there are a few people hovering, will my leathery carcass be found draped over the kitchen table one day? It's an effort to do anything positive, especially listing "fors" and "againsts" of selling a dream. I read indecisiveness can be caused by the fear of making mistakes… a feature of perfectionism. Just go for it, one way or the other? But then I think about your constant advice, Colin: 'If you don't know what to do, don't do anything.' When A sold her cottage she said, 'I simply had to harden myself and walk away. You have to do the same.' N said, 'I loved my house when my husband was alive. Now I want to move - but I haven't a clue where I want to go. I just can't figure myself out. I'm lonely - but I don't want to live with anyone. What a muddle I'm in.' Join the club! The trouble is, Colin, I think I've become the social loner I was afraid of growing into when we first moved here. Fields, trees, sumptuous skies, rabbits, birds and moles have become my constant companions. And as for spring here - it really is paradise. I can't believe I'm writing this! It was you who longed to get away from it all, not me. You were right, there is no escaping the seasons. If we live close to Nature, we become part of it. Your passion for the environment has turned me green, too. I'll be curing warts next.

Of course, I was hoping for a miracle, wasn't I? Everything sorting itself out without too much effort on my part. It had happened once before in my life when I was leaving College for the last time. I hated the thought because I'd been so happy there, but when the moment came I couldn't wait to get away. Every student except me had left but I'd caught mumps and was not allowed to travel by train, and we didn't have a car. I rattled around in silent studies until my Dad rolled up on his bike. He'd cycled over sixty miles from Derby. I mistakenly thought he'd come to take me home. And he guessed it. He hired a taxi to take us to Derby. I know he couldn't afford it. I've never forgotten.

As well as us continually arguing (except when he was training me to be a sprinter when I obeyed him implicitly) he would suddenly do something so magnanimous I'd feel deep love and gratitude.

Then we'd be arguing again!

Saturday: I had a nightmare last night and woke up screaming. As I woke, I thought, I'll wake everyone up. Truly in my dreams.

Sunday: Determined to make the most of myself for lunch date with man from Cruse who said I was his type. Alas, I developed a cold sore. Spent even longer doing up my face. Glanced in the car mirror before I sashayed towards him. One eye was blood-shot. Dracula's daughter, no less. Foolishly offered to pay for half of the meal... he carefully worked out who'd had what drinks and what I owed him. Don't think I'm "his type" after all. But we are going to a lecture together - if I can afford it.

The following day I took the RoSPA advanced driving test. I filled up with petrol, cleaned and polished the car and prized pebbles out of tyres. Wished Colin were there to support me. Don't be daft, I told myself, if Colin were here you wouldn't be driving his car. It was sheeting down with rain. I was as horribly nervous as before a race.

'The very worst thing in your life has happened to you already. Nothing can ever be as bad again,' I said defiantly. It didn't work.

My examiner was a large cuddly Teddy Bear of a man who presented a straight face throughout.

To start, I forgot to do the brake test. At the first main road I sat dithering too long, waiting for a space in traffic. At least it gave me a chance to clear the misty windscreen. Why the hell do I put myself through this? I thought. But I knew why. I wanted to be a good driver. To drive Colin's car superbly.

'Reverse into that car-park,' said the examiner after we had driven for a while (him writing notes).

That was OK. I'd done it before on training runs when the instructor and I stopped to discuss how I was doing. I reversed and turned off the ignition.

'Why have you stopped?' he asked.

'Aren't we going to have a little chat?'

'Chat? You're supposed to be taking a test!'

We stopped next on an incline and he complained I didn't use the hand brake. I can hold a car on a pimple. I have never let a car slide backwards. But it lost me marks.

'Do you realise you actually took your hand off the wheel and changed gear as you drove round a corner?' he remarked after it was all over.

I honestly didn't remember anything at all. I was just glad to get back at the starting point. I'd mugged up on a lot of questions - stuff about nylon tights and drive-belts. I managed to babble on when he asked me about everything except tights and drive-belts.

It seemed he was undecided about failing me but squeezed me into bronze level. He said I suffered considerably with test nerves (as I'd wet myself you could say he was a good judge of character).

'But you will have to retake the test in a year's time,' he warned me.

Laughing with the utmost relief, I assured him that would present no problem whatsoever. No problem.

I was immensely proud of the card that announced I was a tested driver. I'd learned a tremendous lot - enough to emphasise what a hazard I'd been on the road, driving so soon after Colin died.

Thursday: Lovely surprise! I was gardening when Paul rolled up on his hefty motorbike. He followed me to the Rising Sun at Coltishall.

'You don't take many prisoners, mum,' he grunted.

'But the road ahead was clear.'

I knew it all, now.

Sunday: Typical Sunday. Painted the boiler, outside chimney and bedroom ceiling.

Knackered.

Days were busy-busy. One Wednesday after F.I.T. I came home feeling happier than for ages. Everyone had been so friendly. The atmosphere was really great. And I felt I might be getting myself together at last instead of being totally pathetic.

I had "highs" like this. Experience should have taught me to watch out for the drop. But I went on to make the most awful gaffe.

I was invited to supper with a small group of devout people, smiling and friendly, delightful house, Val Doonican music playing soothingly in the background. After a delicious meal conversation, unwisely perhaps, veered towards religion and God breathing life into the first human beings in the Garden of Eden.

At that stage I had the sense to keep my views to myself. But not for long. Sometimes I'm exactly like my dad and can't keep my mouth shut. In hindsight I am amazed that, struggling with my Faith as I was then, I didn't have the gumption to stay silent. But unprepared to listen to doctrinal statements from those whose beliefs shone brightly before them... perhaps I envied them their complete assurance... my stomach knotted when the subject turned to the Virgin Birth. I was having doubts about this, too. And I crassly declared them.

The sudden silence was broken by: 'Oh, you naughty girl!'

'No! Not naughty. Different to you, maybe...' I flared.

Conversation collapsed. Table cleared quickly.

I drove home tearfully. My heart was breaking for Colin. To talk. To discuss issues as we'd often done. I knew what he would have said but imagining it wasn't the same.

I couldn't sleep. Sure I had the right to my opinions just as they did, but I'd struck at the very heart of their Christian beliefs. How I must have hurt them, I thought. Whyever had I gone?

The next day I rang to apologise for upsetting them. The host was generous and gentle and said he was glad I'd felt able to express myself so freely.

So I wasn't worried when I saw them, once more, at a public function. Defending one's corner alone is just another aspect of widowhood. Is biting the tongue as well?

Monday: Readings from Angus Wilson at University of East Anglia. At the bar afterwards, my companion of the tight wallet said, 'Do you like Saki?' I thought he meant the drink. 'No,' I said. He replied solemnly, 'Too cruel?'

25th May: Painted more ceilings and walls. Spent days sorting out my tax. Apparently I owe £560 in back tax. The estate agent wants to talk to me about the cottage. I will not be pressurised. It's my life, my home.

13th June: The cottage is exquisitely beautiful at this time of the year. It seduces me over and over. Baby rabbits romp about the lawn; flash of bronze as a fox slides through sugar-beet; squirrels scamper; deer frolic ahead of Tamba and me in the loke; pigeons coo softly. There is no place like this anywhere.

June: Joined other widows at a Family and Friends Masonic lunch. Excellent meal, pleasant company, flowers to take home. A Brother approached me, 'We nearly put you widows at a table on your own,' he said.

20th June: My article, Why It's Best To Face It Together, was published in the paper with a photograph of members. A chain dangling around my neck gave the impression of a cleavage. I wish. My breasts have withered. (The article brought a wide response from bereaved people wanting to know about us, or to simply talk.)

Sunday: A marvellous day. Daphne opened her home at Cromer to members of F.I.T. and we had a wonderful ploughman's lunch. Our cars set off for Cromer with one man leading. Soon there was a large queue behind us. He'd seen a pheasant waddling slowly across the road and left passengers to carefully escort it across. After a round of applause we set off again.

What food! Cheeses, salads, pickles, strawberries and cream, fruit-salad, homemade cakes and wine. The charge of two pounds each left money over for funds. After lunch a few snoozed in the sunny garden while the rest of us walked to Cromer lighthouse. On the way back, Wally bought us all ice creams, which we ate, sitting in a line on a wall. Back for tea and talking. The day shines like a beacon in the year. A time for healing. For putting ourselves first and learning to care again.

TWENTY-SEVEN

17th July 1992: I am going on holiday on my own for the first time. Received programme for the Writers' Summer School at Swanwick in Derbyshire. It looks very full and quite marvellous. Colin would be so pleased I'm doing this. But how will it be, not having him around afterwards to tell him all about it?

18th July: Drove to Blakeney. Piercing blue sky and pom-pom clouds. There it was I scattered Colin's ashes two years ago. In the sea and under the sun where lines on beached yachts thrummed; where flags flapped in soft breezes. Where he did his last painting. I drove home between gold-matted fields daubed with hay-rolls. How close to you I feel my love.

30th July: Yesterday I gloss-painted my first door. It looked like crepe paper. Martin arrived, stripped it and showed me a better way to do it. Took me for a spin in his M.G. Fantastic! I loved it. He gave me a book called, "Do it!" A guide to living your dreams, by John-Roger and Peter McWilliams. He always leaves me feeling inspired.

Monday: I've found it easier to paint ceilings using a roller attached to a broom handle. Painted kitchen walls and windows and picked raspberries. Invasion of black beetles under the back door. Rang the District Council. They don't come out for beetles. 'They've got a right to be outside your door, madam, when you think about it.'

'It's inside I don't want them.'

Found it very upsetting to have to spray under the door. They really have got rights.

July 1992: Am rethinking attitudes:

1. No man compares with Colin so I have to learn to adjust to life on my own.

2. Discipline myself to write regularly again as when doing serials. It is the only time I am truly absorbed.

3. Mix with more people - and not only the widowed.

4. Listen to my inner voice. There is no rush to sell the cottage. I can stay here as long as I feel like it... but a more positive approach. I shall look at properties for sale to see again what it is I don't want. I shall try to take one day at a time without being anxious about the future.

5. Know I have the right to be indecisive.

July: My Income Tax details have now been passed on to Tyne and Wear. How ridiculous to send them to the other end of the country. Was on the phone to them for twenty minutes. (Peak time.) Explained I was paying twice on untaxed Post-Office interest. That I'd already paid a lump sum. She finally remarked, 'I can't get you to grasp it.' Cheek! It eventually transpired we were talking at cross-purposes. She suddenly piped up, 'Have you closed your Post-Office account?' 'Yes!' I almost shrieked. 'Unfortunately, you didn't say so on your Tax-Return.' How I hate Income Tax forms.

A F.I.T. member asked me if I'd like to go to a barbecue with him.

'But I'm not driving my car along your loke,' he said.

At the barbecue, an acquaintance from the village said, 'I'm not surprised he won't take his new car down there.'

'Colin drove along it four times a day and he didn't have any bother,' I exclaimed.

'That's not what he told me. He told me it broke thirteen springs on his car and I shouldn't attempt to drive down there.'

Colin Sutton, you fibber!

But it made me laugh so, because I remembered how he'd grin and tease, 'Never let the truth get in the way of a good story.'

Wednesday: Norfolk and Norwich hospital for another examination of arthritic hip. Saw a young American doctor. He read my notes and asked me what HRT was.

30th July: A man came to stain the window frames and slapped some over the old paint. I mustered my courage to tell him to take it all off and do it properly.

8th August: It seems like yesterday you died, my Colin. But it's two and a half years. I went for a walk and met J who lost his wife just before you died. He said he'd found a heap of birthday cards and cried into them. Then he said, 'I asked myself, who am I crying for? My wife, or myself?' He looked at me solemnly, 'She's OK. Colin's OK. We cry for ourselves.'

Saturday: I don't want to go to Swanwick after all. I want to stay in the cottage. Whatever made me imagine I would be happy going anywhere on my own?

But I did go to Swanwick. Very reluctantly. The next entry in my diary reads:

30th August 1992: Returned home from Swanwick. Such an exhilarating, informative, amazing time!

On the first day I felt so strange, although everyone was lovely. I had to keep going back to my snug little room to be alone. So many people chattering and laughing overwhelmed me. I was a "white badge" because I was new and was very much in awe of the "yellow badges," some of whom had been going there for years. But I settled in.

The folk in the Garden House where I slept were so friendly (would the posh new building have been such fun?). And I discovered this was one type of holiday where it didn't matter a scribble if you were on your own. Everyone had something in common - writing. I think a mutual interest holiday is the very best sort of holiday for anyone going it alone. We talked about writing, attended daily lectures, had discussions... every day was so full there was no time to think about anything else - especially one's state of being.

I particularly enjoyed a marvellous lecture given by Mavis Nicholson who urged us to spin our own yarn before it's too late. I thought, I must carry on writing about how I feel since Colin died. Perhaps others might identify with my problems and know they aren't alone.

After watching the hilarious midweek pantomime written each year by a Swanwick writer and acted by writers, I shuffled shyly to the dancing hut. Before I knew what was happening, I was in a great squash, jigging and disco dancing with a journalist called Jack. Suddenly, it hit me like a stack of books.

I was dancing.

I WAS LAUGHING!

TWENTY-EIGHT

The first years after Colin died brought searing pain, eternal searching and perpetual longing. I thought I was changed forever. There would never be a time when I would cease to love and want him. But, little by little, I would learn to cope with that pain.

'Time will heal you know.'

I hated that platitude well-meaning friends had murmured. But, unbelievably, it did.

The years to follow would be a testing time. On good days I'd tell myself that the everlasting problems were character-building and there to be solved. On bad days, I'd snivel and pound and shout, 'Why me?'

In September 1993, I became Chairperson of Norwich Writers' Circle. I asked Colin to be with me when I went to Chair my first meeting, stepping gingerly across the gravel in dainty white high heels and slinky frock.

I never did stop talking to him. I knew what his answers would be, and that, had he still been alive, he would have been sitting proudly at the meeting with me. Despite fearful nerves it went OK and everyone was very kind. Late that night I danced across the patio towards the cottage, deliriously pleased to have the first meeting over.

I opened the front door. Water cascaded from the hallway into the outside porch. I stared, bewildered. There was an enormous boom and more dirty water swirled around me. I took off my shoes and paddled in, open-mouthed.

The solid fuel boiler had burst. Got its own back hadn't it after all that belly beating. I turned off the main stopcock; Colin had shown me where it was often enough - tucked behind a panel in the back porch. I didn't know if this would stop water spouting from the central heating system - but it was all I could think of.

I hurriedly tucked my dress up and spent the next three hours filling buckets and slinging water into the garden. The dog leapt in and out like a child at the seaside. Twice, when I thought I'd made inroads into the black river of sludge, the boiler exploded again and more torrents burst forth.

'Why didn't you ring us? We would have come and helped you?' said friends later. It sounds easy - ring friends. But they've got to be bosom at that time of night. And relatives were a thousand million miles away.

I finally crawled up to bed at three a.m. Half an hour later I knew without doubt I was having a heart attack.

The young woman doctor was exceptional. For a start she found the cottage without any problems... brilliant map-reader. She sat with me for a long time, talking quietly and patiently. Slowly my pulse stopped racing and what turned out to be a panic attack subsided. She was in no hurry to leave me alone, even though it was leaning towards dawn. I will forever be grateful to her. I still shudder when I remember that midnight flood.

Being alone in a crisis stinks.

23rd February 1994: Any Questions at F.I.T. with our members on the panel. One man's answer, with a twinkle in his eye, included the remark, 'Don't you remember those Sunday afternoons in bed with The News Of The World?'

216

Everyone exploded with laughter. We're all getting better together I thought.

26th June 1994: Tonight I feel at one with the cottage. The summer sky at ten p.m. is streaked pale pink and apricot behind a lacy fretwork of apple and plum trees. The scent of orange-blossom competes with herbs Colin planted under the windows. Ribes are full-leafed and developing purple berries.

Not as though everything in the garden is honeyed sweetness. This morning at five o'clock a multitude of magpies hammered relentlessly at putty on my bedroom window until I flung it open. If it isn't them disturbing sleep, it's pea-scarers or pigeons, or squirrels that rape my nut trees.

Finally, but not cruelly, I have caught my mole. There are so many mole-heaps on the lawn. Goodbye Wind In The Willows. I've had enough of Moley and Ratty. Toady can stay. Whenever I put Tamba out at night, I must carry a family of three toads to where she can't bark them to death. But they always return. So do cows that munch into the garden.

I remember when you phoned a farmer, Colin, when his cows were snuffling at our windows one dark night.

'Cows?' said the farmer, in the way they do. 'Cows? What cows are them, then?'

'They're big and brown with a leg in each corner,' you replied dryly.

Aren't I going on? Tonight this place has got to me. I feel your presence, Colin. Here, we have watched hares cavorting in the wind and red foxes shooting streamlined over fields. Remember flocks of seagulls swooping behind tractors? And how amused we were when pheasants strutted boldly on the first day of the closed season.

Here we have stooked beans, picked berries, collected rose hips and gathered holly. And watched green shoots grow into waving golden rye.

And each year turning on its axis has been wondrous.

How soon I forget the not so romantic - the hard graft of rebuilding a cottage. Demolishing, wheeling and tipping. Paul tackling heavy "bum" jobs, a younger Martin covered from helmet to boots in thick grey dust ('Gets right up your nose, dad') and Seán balanced cloud-high, swaying and sawing through monster branches of trees. And everyone back-filling and more back-filling. A far cry lads from the land of rock-music, guitars and motorbikes. And we had, and I still have, the right to be proud of you.

I got so used to you dressed in torn jumpers and safety-pinned trousers, Colin, you turned me on all over again when you wore your suit. And didn't you know it? You lady-killer, you.

And by the way, there's another darned wasps' nest under the eaves.

21st September 1994: Ten of us from F.I.T. went on a Cruiser on the Broads from Wroxham to Ranworth. Oh, it was a lovely day! Like sailing in a big watercolour painting. I think the owner thought I was a nerd demanding life jackets before we set off. Well, we aren't spring chickens and every year people get drowned on the Broads.

We only bumped another boat when we moored to have our picnics.

We carried on from the Bure along the Ant, watching herons, black swans, Chinese geese, coots and more... I felt refreshed and peaceful. We all had a go at the wheel. When we moored to walk to the remains of St. Benet's Abbey, an old monastery, we swung out too far into the river. One of our seventy-year olds leapt on to the bank and pulled us in with help from a young guy in a sailor-hat.

'I'll give you half-a-crown for your hat,' called Wally.

'What's half-a-crown?' replied the lad.

We sailed back to base singing heartily.

If I die tonight, I have enjoyed today and lived it to the full. And there is one moment I shall remember especially. When we were singing, I remarked on P's beautifully sweet voice. She said she had sung a lot when her husband had been alive.

'This is the first time I've sung since he died,' she said.

An acquaintance of ours, who belonged to one of the same associations as Colin, called to see me. It was a fairly general chat. Then before he left, he unexpectedly gave me a full smacking kiss on the lips. I was appalled. Naively, I wondered if I'd misunderstood. Perhaps he was simply being paternally kind. But I was staggered; I felt vulnerable and didn't know how to handle it.

If it happened to me now I'd tell him to piss off.

24th November 1994: My birthday. Drove to Derby. Left my car in Little Chef car park after activating the alarm. Drank several cups of coffee, went to the toilet and managed to drop my car alarm key into the lavatory pan. Even after drying it under the hand-drier, it would not de-activate the alarm so I had to phone the AA.

'I'm a woman on my own - my sister is expecting me.' I felt like adding, 'And it's my birthday.'

The AA suggested I return to the restaurant for a cup of coffee while they sent someone out. I had another go with the hand-drier - dried every little part of the alarm very thoroughly. This time it worked. I now carry a spare battery. And I am not so slap-dash, either.

In December, Paul and Julie had a son. My first grandchild. A little darling. When I first held him in my arms I cried. What do you expect?

27th December 1994: Into hospital for a Prolapse operation. Didn't like it. Especially at visiting time. But I wrote a story about it and won a hundred pounds and a trophy in a competition.

This inspired me to get on with the writing and I didn't have the need to pour my soul into diaries. I was too busy.

5th January 1996: Developed pneumonia after flu. Drove back from surgery with supply of antibiotics and crawled into bed.

6th January: My dear little 92 year old mum fell down the stairs and was taken to hospital

8th January: Martin came up from Chesham for a few days to look after me. It was like seeing God.

The illness continued for weeks. I'd cry, 'I can't cope!' Hard luck, folks. We just have to grit our teeth and get on with it.

26th January 1996: Spent an hour with a homeopathic doctor. He swung a pendulum, murmuring mysteriously to himself and stuck minute white tablets upon my person with sellotape. Felt like the princess and the pea as I walked around Tesco limping with a tablet under my foot.

After that visit to the homeopath I unexpectedly felt much more at peace with myself - I think it was because he took so much time with me - although it was a long time before I felt physically stronger. I drove home that day through a blinding snowstorm on icy roads. My front nearside wheel collided with the kerb before I steered into the skid and gained control. At my friendly Crown Garage, David said I should keep an eye on the tyre for bulges.

'Wow, look at that lot.' We gazed towards the A140 where queues of cars were driving painfully slowly. I was nearly home when I skidded again at a junction. There was only one other car near me and that was upside down in a ditch.

27th January 1996: Drifts in loke. I am snowed in. Looks beautiful like Switzerland. And so peaceful. Have fed the birds and Tamba and am content to settle down and write.

TWENTY-NINE

TOWARDS RECOVERY:

When I was feeling inconsolable, I cried and cried and sometimes I prayed. All was blackness. No hope whatsoever. Then, emotionally drained and limp as a wet sock, I'd shuffle off to kitchen and kettle. Only once did I hit the bottle. But I felt so dreadful the following day, I avoided repeating the procedure.

Every one of us reacts differently. We cannot know how another feels. Barbara used to press her face into her husband's jacket to try and revive the smell of him; Ron had his lunches in a pub so he was not alone all day; Marion immersed herself in books; Emma painted a room, bit by little bit. Vera said, 'We've just got to get on with it, haven't we?'

The following were therapeutic for me at varying stages of bereavement:

Talking (big telephone bills ahead but I economised by buying my clothes in Charity shops).

Keeping busy... anything. I'd slouch into the garden, pull up a weed, then another - and soon, an hour would disappear. I avoided sunset... all that stuff about walking into, hand-in-hand. I knew I was getting better when I didn't sob into my trowel every time the sky turned red.

Indoors I'd paint a door or re-arrange furniture. Or slump in front of television whatever was on and drink lots of tea... but then, making tea was "doing".

I walked the dog. Near people. Scenery is not for the sad. Although I did eventually reach the stage where I found great peace in my silent surroundings. That was after the screaming inside me had stopped.

I was warned not to make big decisions for a year after Colin died (or "promoted" as Michael Bentine told me). Chance would be a fine thing! I was Mrs Indecision herself.

When I made the effort to go to a Sports Centre, I found swimming wonderfully relaxing. And no one could spot the tears. Afterwards I'd spend a couple of hours in the restaurant reading the paper and drinking coffee (murdered my bladder).

I read how it is beneficial to smile into the mirror every morning. Pretend to be happy. Some folk fake this one so well everyone thinks they are fine again. I didn't. I sought help. From anyone. Anywhere.

I had to learn not to be too sensitive. G said I could stay with her whenever I felt miserable or lonely. She added, 'I was only thinking the other day, I wanted to do something... and I don't subscribe to any charity.' It's true people often don't know what to say to a bereaved person - but they always mean well.

I took sleeping tablets for a while then borrowed a marvellous relax-ation tape which helped me sleep. I also tried herbal capsules.

Few of us sleep when we lose our partners. In fact I still wake and wander in the night and brew up tea. Or listen to talk radio.

I acquired a big basic DIY book. And every time someone recommended a good and trustworthy plumber/handyman/decorator, I'd put name and telephone no. in a WHO TO CALL envelope.

I learned not to whittle about imperfections. If it looks passable, if it works, leave it.

Expect some folk to knock you off their Christmas-card list the second year. The first year it's sympathy.

I junked stuff. Iris and I sold a load of rubbish at a boot-sale on a lovely sunny day. It was fun. The nicest part was getting out and being among people. Many widowed give partners' clothes to charity. I still have one jacket of Colin's. I'm told it's not good to hang on to it. I'll decide that.

When I kicked out of apathy it gave me a buzz if I did something stimulating, like driving lessons, attending adult education classes, starting a group or listening (and moving... even on a chair) to loud lively music.

I found a good garage p.d.q.

One of the biggest "downs" for me was being ill on my own. Unless you are very old or very ill, I don't believe the National Health Service wants to know once you leave hospital. I put a television in the bedroom but on the whole it was a question of gritting the teeth and getting better. A bedside telephone is a must. If we need help in the house and have any money, this is the time to spend our children's inheritance.

I rushed into buying a puppy when my dog died, just after Colin. I found her unbelievably exhausting at a time when I was continually tired anyway. If I had not been so isolated I would have waited longer.

Sara chose her dog from the RSPCA shortly after she was widowed; this match did not work out and she, too, became very tired. She returned the dog and was matched with another far more suitable and they lived happily for years. A dog involves work and walking and can be a tie, but it takes away biting loneliness and can, like other creatures, become a treasured companion.

I read it was a good idea to do something you're scared of. Come to think of it, I was pretty well scared of everything. My driving instructor said I drove as if I was waiting for someone to jump out at me and shout, "Boo!". That pretty well sums it up. Do it for Colin, I'd bribe myself. That usually worked. I am more self-confident now. Last year, when Seán and his partner Annalisa were staying with me while they waited for visas to Australia, he finally persuaded me to get a computer and taught me how to use it (no easy task!) But I'm so pleased he did. I love it. It keeps my brain moving - and it's company.

Sometimes after a bereavement it is simply getting out of the house that scares us or breaking down in front of people or walking into a room where we don't know anybody. It happens to all of us. But nothing really matters does it? Only life and death matter. And biding our time until the pining and the pain ease up and we can rejoin the parade before it passes by for us as well.

Our Facing It Together groups are a lifeline. They're all about contact. Mini-groups are formed, friendships cemented, holiday outings and lunches arranged. The emptiness we feel after a loss is dreadful. No one can know until it happens to him or her. Last week a new member at F.I.T. said, 'I knew that whoever I sat by would have gone through what I've gone through. Would understand.'

Anyone can start such a group.

YOU CAN!

And don't think it's gloom incorporated. It isn't! The chattering has to be heard to be believed. One day we had a talk on gardening. I asked the question:

'My pear trees grow little pears but they all drop off. Why?'

'What your trees lack, my dear, is a sex-life.'

'Don't we all,' I replied.

There was uproar. But of course, for many widowed, it is true. I have had sexual experiences since Colin died, but I miss the permanence and comfy familiarity which grew out of a thirty-five year relationship. It is not easy starting the mating game again. It's certainly very different to when I was a teenager. Not many women then carried condoms or had to worry about AIDS.

But I ain't the only one living alone and that's for sure.

It was healing for me to write again... a diary to start with. And letters and poems to Colin. And I am absolutely sure that, had he been in my position, he would have painted constantly.

A friend went on a painting holiday and met her future partner there. Activity holidays are great for singles. So, says one of our members, are Saga holidays. I store holiday leaflets to browse through in a "Keeping Sane" file, with notices from clubs and societies. Never mind if you've not been interested in "The Life of the Lugworm" before. Go to the talk and meet people.

I had lost a life-style and had to learn new ways of living. It made sense to me, as a woman alone, to take certain precautions, like a phone in the car for times I travelled long distances. I was interested to read about the male dummy that could be unfolded from a suitcase and positioned beside the woman driver at night. Better than dressing up a mop-head on a stick as my sister does. At the moment I'm looking for a blow-up doll with a guarantee against deflating at the worst moments.

Sometimes even friends avoid sad people because they don't know what to say to them. Words can be so inadequate, can't they? My lovely little mum met a newly widowed lady on the bus, gently squeezed her arm as she passed and said, 'Look after yourself.' It was as simple as that. On our part, we should not be afraid to ask for help. Ever.

Losing a beloved partner changes us. But life goes on. I have seen new members of F.I.T. who arrive pale and unhappy, joining in with the activities and smiling as weeks progress, even joking. The brave widow who broke both her wrists told me she couldn't put her knickers on for a fortnight: 'My neighbour left a message to tell me not to do hand-stands,' she chuckled.

Once we could not lock up after the meeting because J was chattering so much. That day she'd been given a lift by one of our Senior Citizen members. When she rang him to see when he was collecting her she heard his grandson shout: 'It's your bird, granddad.'

There will come a time to laugh again!

AND FINALLY

I lived alone in Colin's Cottage for six years. The first two were the worst. By the sixth year I was pretty much in love with the place.

Arthritis finally limited the wielding and whooshing of rip hooks. Weeds turned into trees while lawns waited for two hasty lads with mowers.

Those lovely big rooms we'd coveted were expensive to heat for one person. In later years I switched to oil-fired central heating and kicked myself I hadn't done it before, even if the tanker did always seem to arrive in bad weather gouging out great channels in the muddy loke. Out again with the spade!

Because of Facing It Together I now knew many people in Aylsham and felt, at least, I wouldn't be a stranger in a strange land if I moved there. It's a delightful little market town. And how amazing to be able to walk out at night under the yellow glow of lamps; to have milk and papers delivered... and no more trudging in wellingtons to a distant bus-stop. (My suburban self showing?)

Nevertheless, it was the hardest decision of all. To leave Colin's Cottage.

I now live where I can push a wheelie-bin along a neat uncluttered drive next to other neat uncluttered drives. No more dumping refuse bags in ripe heaps for collection every three weeks.

I've become caught up with a variety of activities. I have read for The Mardler, the newspaper sent out on cassette for the blind; enjoy Extend keep-fit after a successful hip operation, and perform annually in the local pantomime. It's fun to be tapped on the shoulder by strangers and asked: 'Excuse me, are you Wishy-Washy?'

I could now drive blindfold to Derbyshire where our beloved mother aged ninety-six, is in her gentle twilight years.

Cancer clobbered my ninety year old father one Christmas but could never quell his indomitable spirit. We shall never see the like of him again. On the morning after his funeral we found these words traced on the frosty car windscreen: "Hell was full so I came back". Any practical joker (and I don't want to believe it was) sure knew my dad's sense of humour!

And I miss him.

I have started more Facing It Together groups. One even has a waiting list. Its members holiday together all over the place, including a jaunt to Paris. I doubt many of them stay home for long. I have met so many lovely people through these clubs.

Jack Barfoot, the kind and clever journalist I met at Swanwick (another place for forming friendships) often visits me while I belong to his Writers' Circle in Surrey as well as Norwich Writers' Circle.

Soon I shall journey on my own to Australia to visit Annalisa and Seán, who is an Internet Developer in Perth.

But between all the frenetic activity I love spending valuable and peaceful time in my small easily manageable herb-filled garden.

Making it look countrified!

No time then, to mourn? No missing my cottage? I'd be lying if I said I didn't miss it. I have walked along the loke... only once... to try and kill ghosts. Leaving had been like another bereavement.

In my imagination I shall always see it clearly - two smooth boulders on either side of the cottage to keep witches out (I shouldn't have moved those boulders). The door was off-centre, too, so the devil couldn't find the entrance. But he did.

When the cottage was built, wheat was seven shillings and a farthing a bushel. The Cromer road was a Turnpike. We found an iron rim from a carriage wheel in the garden and old silver sixpences under window sills.

It was all a dream come true for Colin. And I grew to love it as much as he knew I would.

Children born and bred in the country are lucky indeed - but you can bet, when puberty strikes, they'll be off to where they don't have to catch the last bus home early, or to where they are accessible to friends with bed rolls strapped permanently to backs.

But in later years, when mists glide through tinted leaves and it is time to plough again after harvest, will minds wander back to a rural Utopia?

I hope, wherever our children travel in their busy lives, they will find a measure of tranquillity that is to be found in the long green grass.

I know one thing for sure. If Colin came back and asked me to go with him to the most outlandish of places, no power - on earth - would stop me.

THE LIFE THAT I HAVE

By: LEO MARKS

The life that I have
Is all that I have
And the life that I have
Is yours

The love that I have
Of the life that I have
Is yours and yours and yours

A sleep I shall have
A rest I shall have
Yet death will be but a pause

For the peace of my years
In the long green grass
Will be yours and yours and yours

THE END